WOODCRAFT

BY

NESSMUK

(GEORGE W. SEARS)

FIRST PUBLISHED IN 1884

LEGACY EDITION

LIBRARY OF AMERICAN OUTDOORS CLASSICS

BOOK 2

FEATURING

REMASTERED CLASSIC WORKS OF THE HIGHEST QUALITY FROM
THE TIMELESS MASTERS AND TEACHERS OF CAMPING, OUTDOORS
SKILLS, WOODCRAFT, AND TRADITIONAL HANDCRAFTS

Doublebit Press
Eugene, OR

*This book is part of the **Doublebit Library of American Outdoors Classics** toward*
preserving the knowledge and skills of the American outdoors tradition.

This title, along with other Doublebit Press books including the Library of
American Outdoors Classics, are available at a volume discount for outdoors
clubs or reading groups. Doublebit Press titles are available for youth groups to
sell via fundraisers. Contact Doublebit Press at info@doublebitpress.com for
more information.

Doublebit Press Legacy Edition ISBNs
Hardcover: 978-1-64389-005-0
Paperback: 978-1-64389-004-3

First Doublebit Press Legacy Edition Printing, 2019

Printed in the United States of America
when purchased at retail in the USA

INTRODUCTION
To The Doublebit Press Legacy Edition

George Washington Sears, known better under his penname of *Nessmuk*, stood at a strong 5 feet, 3 inches, and 103 pounds. Finding solace in the woods due to his tuberculosis and asthma, he found himself a solo canoe that he named the *Sairy Gimp* and traveled the Adirondacks in America. He was inspired much by William Henry Harrison Murray's *Adventures in the Wilderness*, which is probably the first "camping" book that was published in the states. Drawing energy from Murray's descriptions of the wilds and his promotion of health and well-being from getting out of the city, Nessmuk quickly became an expert of the outdoors.

After hearing all the old tales of the trappers, woodsmen, and visitors of the wilds, Nessmuk penned this book, *Woodcraft*. First published in 1884, Nessmuk's *Woodcraft* represents the first "how-to" manual of the woods and camp life, seconded in popularity perhaps only by Horace Kephart's *Book of Camping and Woodcraft*. Nessmuk also shared his outdoors-inspired poetry in a book called *Forest Runes* (1897). Nessmuk died at his home in Pennsylvania in 1904.

Perhaps Nessmuk's most famous line from this book represents the relative ease of visiting the outdoors as your temporary home: "We do not go to the woods to rough it; we go to smooth it — we get it rough enough in town. But let us live the simple, natural life in the woods, and leave all frills behind." Instead of it being *harder* without the conveniences of modern life, life outdoors should be easier and restore us to our true selves. We shouldn't work hard to be outside – we work hard every day in city life and careers. We go outside to truly unwind.

This present edition is a facsimile reprint of the twelfth printing (1900). Its volumes have been consistently reprinted throughout the twentieth and twenty-first centuries, lending the tidbits, tricks, and tales of the wilds to many generations. Enjoy this handbook by the Dean of the Outdoors – there's a ton of information to glean from its pages!

About the Legacy Editions of the Library of American Outdoors Classics

The old experts of the woods and mountains taught timeless principles and skills for decades. Through their books, the old experts offered rich descriptions of the outdoor world and encouraged learning through personal experiences in nature. Over the last 125 years, camping, outdoors recreation, and woods activities have substantially changed. Many things have gotten simpler as gear has improved, and life outside or on the trail now brings with it many of the same comforts enjoyed in town. In addition, some activities of the olden days are now no longer in vogue, or are even outright considered inappropriate or illegal, such as high-impact camping practices like chopping down live trees. However, despite many of the positive changes in outdoors methods that have occurred over the years, *there are many other skills and much knowledge that have been forgotten* from the golden era of American outdoors recreation.

By publishing the Library of American Outdoors Classics, it is our goal at Doublebit Press to do what we can to preserve and share the works from forgotten teachers that form the cornerstone of the history of the American outdoors. Through remastered reprint editions of timeless classics of outdoor recreation, perhaps we can regain some of this lost knowledge for future generations.

Because there were fewer options for finding outdoors gear in the early 1900's, experts in *"woodcraft"* skills (not to be confused with today's use of the word to mean woodworking or making things of wood) had to have a deep knowledge of the basic building blocks of outdoor living. This involved not only surviving in the outdoors, but to also have a comfortable and enjoyable time. As Nessmuk puts it in his book *Woodcraft,* "We do not go to the woods to rough it; we go to smooth it — we get it rough enough in town. But let us live the simple, natural life in the woods, and leave all frills behind." Nessmuk did not advocate for folks to go outside and have a terrible time. That would be contrary to the whole point of getting outside. Instead, he advocated for a "simpler" life by leaving some of the creature comforts of the city behind, but also entering the outdoors in a smart and practiced way that made the experience a much more satisfying vacation from home. The goal is to be comfortable so you can focus on having a good time outside and take in everything exposure to nature can offer. However, to be comfortable, one has to know the ins and outs of camping and outdoors life. Despite all the advances in campcraft and outdoors recreation, the old masters of the woods would all likely argue that this will only come from practicing the basics.

Because there was no market yet for specialty outdoors recreational gear (and thus, few outfitters), most outdoors gear came from military surplus piles or was custom made. As such, the old masters of woodcraft often made their own gear suited to their tastes. Through much experience in the woods and field, the great outdoors experts had to know why things worked the way they did by understanding the great web of cause and effect in nature. They had to learn from experience why certain gear worked better in different conditions or know how to solve problems off-the-cuff when things got hairy. They used the basic blocks of camping and outdoors knowledge to fine-tune their gear. They gained experience whenever they could and tried things different ways so they could gain mastery over the fundamentals and see challenges from many angles.

Today, much of the outdoor experience has been greatly simplified by neatly arranged campsites at public campgrounds and gear that has been meticulously improved and tested in both the lab and the field. Many modern conveniences are only a brief trek away, with many parks, campgrounds, and even forests having easy-access roads, convenience stores, and even cell phone signal. In some ways, it is much easier to camp and go outdoors today, and that is a good thing! We should not be miserable when we go outside — lovers of the outdoors know the essential restorative capability that the woods can have on the body, mind, and soul. Although things have gotten easier on us in the 21st Century when it comes to the outdoors, it certainly does not mean that we should forget the foundations of outdoors lore, though. All modern camping skills, outdoors equipment, and cool gizmos that make our lives easier are all founded on principles of the outdoors that the old masters knew well and taught to those who would listen.

Every woods master had their own curriculum or thought some things were more important than others. This includes the present author — certain things appear in this book that other masters leave out of theirs. The old masters also taught common things in slightly different ways or did things differently than others. That's what makes each of the experts different and worth reading. There's no universal way of doing something, especially now. Learning to go about something differently helps with mastery or learn a new skill altogether. Again, to use the metaphor from the above paragraphs, outdoors skills mastery consists of learning the basic building blocks of outdoors living, woods and nature lore, and the art of packing properly for trips. Each master goes about describing these building blocks differently or shows a different aspect of them.

Therefore, we have decided to publish this Legacy Edition in our Library of American Outdoors Classics series. This book is an important contribution to the early American recreational outdoors literature and has important historical and collector value toward preserving the American outdoors tradition. The knowledge it holds is an invaluable reference for practicing skills and hand craft methods. Its chapters thoroughly discuss some of the essential building blocks of knowledge that are fundamental but may have been forgotten as equipment gets fancier and technology gets smarter. In short, this book was chosen for Legacy Edition printing because much of the basic skills and knowledge it contains has been forgotten or put to the wayside in trade for more modern conveniences and methods.

Although the editors at Doublebit Press are thrilled to have comfortable experiences in the woods and love our high-tech and light-weight equipment, we are also realizing that the basic skills taught by the old masters are more essential than ever as our culture becomes more and more hooked on digital stuff. We don't want to risk forgetting the important steps, skills, or building blocks involved with thriving in the outdoors. The Legacy Edition series represents the essential contributions to the American outdoors tradition by the great experts of outdoors life and traditional hand crafting.

With technology playing a major role in everyday life, sometimes we need to take a step back in time to find those basic building blocks used for gaining mastery – the things that we have luckily not completely lost and has been recorded in books over the last two centuries. These skills aren't forgotten, they've just been shelved. *It's time to unshelve them once again and reclaim the lost knowledge of self-sufficiency.*

Based on this commitment to preserving our outdoors and handcraft heritage, we have taken great pride in publishing this book as a complete original work. We hope it is worthy of both study and collection by outdoors folk in the modern era of outdoors and traditional skills life.

Unlike many other photocopy reproductions of classic books that are common on the market, this Legacy Edition does not simply place poor photography of old texts on our pages and use error-prone optical scanning or computer-generated text. We want to have pride in our work on which customers might spend their hard-earned money. With this in mind, each Legacy Edition book that has been chosen for publication is carefully remastered from original print books, *with the Doublebit Legacy Edition printed and laid out in the exact way that it was presented at its original publication.* We provide a beautiful, memorable experience that is as true to the original text as best as possible with modern technology and books that are typically over a century old.

Because of its age, the book may contain misspellings and other errors that were common for the age, which we feel give the book character and were preserved in this Legacy Edition. Each illustration in the text is clean and sharp with the least amount of loss from being copied as possible. Plates are presented as they were found, including the extra blank page that was often behind a plate. For the covers, we use the original cover design to give the book its original feel. All Doublebit Press Legacy Editions are also available as cloth-bound hardcover editions for the serious outdoors collector, which includes a high-quality dust jacket. We are sure you'll appreciate the fine touches and attention to detail that your Legacy Edition has to offer.

For outdoors enthusiasts who demand the best from their equipment, this Doublebit Press Legacy Edition reprint was made with you in mind. Both important and minor details have equally both been accounted for by our publishing staff, down to the cover, font, layout, and images. It is the goal of Doublebit Legacy Edition series to preserve outdoors heritage, but also be cherished as collectible pieces, worthy of collection in any outdoorsperson's library and that can be passed to future generations.

Every book selected to be in this series offers unique views and instruction on important skills, advice, tips, tidbits, anecdotes, stories, and experiences that will enrich the repertoire of any person who enjoys escaping the city and finding their way to the trails of the wilds. To learn the most basic building blocks of outdoors life leads to mastery of all its aspects.

Placing Outdoors Classics Books in Their Historical Times

Enjoying the outdoors is an American tradition! As such, our goal with the Legacy Edition printings of our Library of American Outdoors Classics Series is to preserve this tradition for future generations by preserving the knowledge of the old masters of the craft. Part of enjoying the outdoors today is the need to practice careful stewardship for our wild lands, as well as focus on our own safety. For years, outdoors groups such as the Scouts or sportsmen's associations have taught folks how to enjoy the outdoors and practice traditional skills in a safe and responsible manner. We extend this same challenge to those who read our remastered books.

Authors used to write with a stupendous number of extra words and grand, superfluous prose back in the day! How dreadfully verbose! Some of the words and phrases used by the author, or the views expressed by the author, can also be outdated by today's standards. Because this book was written in a different age, ideas in this text could also be insensitive to some people given today's language use and societal norms. This is not to say that everything in old camping books is politically incorrect (which, of course, it likely is), but instead that it just may sound weird to modern readers.

As such, you should read this book with an idea for the time in which it was written. Language and perspectives change over the centuries. To understand the written knowledge of previous eras, we have to take the language they used in stride and think about what it was like in the early 1900's. We can read historic books within the contexts and times in which they were written. Despite authors perhaps having some outdated social views, these old texts still have plenty to teach and can impart knowledge that has been long lost by today's standards!

In addition to odd language or obsolete ideas, *this book may describe some activities that are incompatible with today's standards of outdoor ethics, consideration for other outdoorspeople, conservation, ecology, and the Leave No Trace philosophy of outdoors recreation.* We can't stress enough: because this book was published decades ago, there are some things in it that are irresponsible, inappropriate, dangerous, or outright illegal today. Forests and forest management have changed a lot since 1900. There is far more caution placed today on the preservation of forests and prevention of fire than in the early 20th Century. Because of this, we caution readers to pay close attention regarding safety, conservation, or legality, particularly include the use of fire, cutting live trees or plants, digging holes, use of firearms or potentially dangerous tools, killing of animals, or activities involving survival in the wilderness, especially when alone. Some activities in this book may even be illegal in some areas, especially public areas such as parks, National Forests, and designated wilderness areas. Even on private property, old outdoors activities and skills can remain dangerous. Any hunting, fishing, or trapping should always be done with proper licenses and training, and within the bounds of the law. When trying new activities from this book, it should be done under the supervision of experts and with a focus on the safety of everyone involved.

We also encourage youth to grab this book and learn from it! Start while you're young! If you're a curious kid or teen who finds the outdoors fascinating and want to become an outdoors expert, the activities in this book should give you a great education in the old woods skills. However, these activities should also be done alongside parents' or qualified adult supervision. We're not trying to be boring or kill the fun - quite the opposite. We believe that youth should have chances to get outside and learn the fun stuff the old woods experts offer to teach in their books. It's just best to consult with adults when doing some of the activities in this book, especially if they are new to you.

It is also useful to check with outdoors stewardship organizations and governments about what outdoors practices are allowed and which are either not or otherwise discouraged. Examples of organizations dedicated to outdoors stewardship include the Leave No Trace Center for Outdoors Ethics, The Mountaineers, The Boy Scouts of America, The Girl Scouts of America, American Hiking Society, Appalachian Mountain Club, Tread Lightly!, and The Sierra Club. Many of these groups' websites have plenty of information about proper outdoors practices and ethics for preserving our great outdoors heritage and lands. Specifically, a visit to your local US Forest Service, Bureau of Land Management, or State Fish and Wildlife Management offices should also point you in the right direction toward questions about regulations, permits, and proper outdoors behavior on public lands.

Finally, Doublebit Press is committed to expanding the access to information for everyone about outdoors mastery, DIY and self-sufficient skills, "simpler" living (said in quotes because the so-called *simple life* can be quite complex), and reflections on the lives of the old master outdoorsfolk. Despite this goal, it is unfortunate that the original texts that we publish most frequently only mention men or boys. It's as if women or girls never wanted to go outside for over a century (hint: it's just not true.) The history of the last two centuries is full of examples of women and girls who found the outdoors restorative, educative, and empowering, such as with the great programs of the Camp Fire Girls and the Girl Scouts. It's an unfortunate aspect of American outdoors history that the outside world was not inviting to everyone. Those who desire to reflect on life's complexities through the simplicity of the outdoors should make this knowledge their own, even if authors were too shortsighted to include everyone in their original texts, or even outright talk down to women who wanted to be outside. We're not trying to be politically correct here, but instead to encourage everyone to get outside and enjoy its benefits.

Studying This Book

The pages within this book present an overwhelming amount of information, facts, and directions to memorize that are often outdated and at the least, out of practice by modern standards. That doesn't mean that these pages have nothing to teach! It's just going to likely be new stuff for many readers.

Our one suggestion is *don't try to memorize everything,* especially when you're thumbing through the book or even reading it cover-to-cover. Writings from the late 1800's to early 1900's can be dense and out of style for someone not used to reading these types of books. Instead, gain some basic familiarity with each topic by thumbing through the pages, looking at the illustrations, and seeing the section headers. Then, choose a few topics or skills at a single time for deeper study.

Before camping or other outdoors trips can even begin, some planning and reflection is useful, which may be best done in town before you go out to the field. First, it might be helpful to read through the book with plans in mind. The book can provide useful material for close study and reflection when in town before you head out to the field to practice.

Secondly, once you've come up with a practice plan, you will of course want to start doing tasks and skills in the field. Doublebit Legacy books and the Library of American Outdoors Classics represents many field skills to master that have long sense been out of practice, but hopefully not forgotten! These include making and trying different kinds of tents or shelters, cooking (including any fish and game caught by you in the field), making many types of fires, setting up camp to suit your personal needs, beating the bugs and elements, understanding the terrain and weather, making furniture, brushing up on your nature lore, emergency survival, and testing your personal outfit and tools.

Any of the old tutors of woodcraft will tell you in their classic books that you can only truly learn how to go camping and do woodcraft by *actually doing it*. Home study indeed does you well by using the many guidebooks that have been published over the previous 125 years. However, hundreds more lessons will become immediately available to you the moment you start with some of the old-style tasks. This old style of outdoorsing is indeed outdated in many ways, but the approach still has much to teach modern campers who have become accustomed to carved out campsites, cabin and RV camping, and high-tech equipment.

Before the days of outfitters, outdoors adventurers made their gear, which was tailored to their individual needs. Many experiments were done in the field to tweak their gear to get that ever-changing point of "perfect." Aside from experiencing wonderful lessons in history, getting outside and doing some of the activities this book will give you an appreciation for modern advances in outdoors and handcraft method and tools of the trade, as well as a deeper understanding of the foundations of outdoors and hand-craft life in the event that your gear fails you or you otherwise find yourself in situations where knowing the principles will get you unstuck fast.

If we were to tally up each of the individual tips in the Doublebit Library of American Outdoors Classics, they would easily number in the thousands. The old masters represent centuries of previous knowledge that have been all but lost to 21st Century, technology-driven folks. To this point, although experience and *actually doing stuff* are the best forms of learning, taking a mindful approach to study of these works also benefit your development as a competent outdoorsperson and handcrafter. You can study alone but working with a friend or travel companion can also help you both learn even more from your companions' experiences!

You may also find it invaluable to take these volumes with you on your camping or other outdoors trips. In addition to having reading material on a variety of topics in the field for down time, you'll also find a thousand things to try in these pages if you're bored. Although skills may be best studied when in the field through experience and reflection, you may also study woods skills at home as well. Gaining familiarity through reading, videos, and other media are a great start toward building your ability toward gaining mastery in the field.

So, without blabbering on further, we hope you enjoy your Doublebit Legacy Edition. May your trails be clear and your experiences be memorable!

- The Doublebit Press Editors

Nessmuk.

WOODCRAFT;

BY

"NESSMUK."

TWELFTH EDITION.

NEW YORK:

FOREST AND STREAM PUBLISHING CO.

1900

CONTENTS.

ILLUSTRATIONS.

PREFACE.

"WOODCRAFT" is dedicated to the Grand Army of "Outers," as a pocket volume of reference on—woodcraft.

For brick and mortar breed filth and crime,
With a pulse of evil that throbs and beats;
And men are withered before their prime
By the curse paved in with the lanes and streets.

And lungs are poisoned and shoulders bowed,
In the smothering reek of mill and mine;
And death stalks in on the struggling crowd—
But he shuns the shadow of oak and pine.

NESSMUK.

WOODCRAFT.

CHAPTER I.

OVERWORK AND RECREATION.—OUTING AND OUTERS. HOW TO DO IT, AND WHY THEY MISS IT.

IT DOES not need that Herbert Spencer should cross the ocean to tell us that we are an overworked nation; that our hair turns gray ten years earlier than the Englishman's; or, "that we have had somewhat too much of the gospel of work," and, "it is time to preach the gospel of relaxation."

It is all true. But we work harder, accomplish more in a given time, and last quite as long as slower races. As to the gray hair—perhaps gray hair is better than none; and it is a fact that the average Briton becomes bald as early as the American turns gray. There is, however, a sad significance in his words when he says, "In every circle I have met men who had themselves suffered from nervous collapse due to stress of business, or named friends who had either killed themselves by overwork, or had been permanently incapacitated, or had wasted long periods in endeavors to recover health." Too true. And it is the constant strain, without let up or relaxation, that, in nine cases out of ten, snaps the chord and ends in what the doctors call "nervous prostration"—something akin to paralysis—from which the sufferer seldom wholly recovers.

Mr. Spencer quotes that quaint old chronicler, Froissart, as saying, "the English take their pleasures sadly, after their fashion;" and thinks if he lived now, he would say of Americans, "they take their pleasures hurriedly, after their fashion." Perhaps.

It is an age of hurry and worry. Anything slower than steam is apt to "get left." Fortunes are quickly made and freely spent. Nearly all busy, hard-worked Americans have an intuitive sense of the need that exists for at least one period of rest and relaxation during each year, and all—or nearly all—are willing to pay liberally, too liberally in fact, for anything that conduces to rest, recreation and sport. I am sorry to say that we mostly get swindled. As an average, the summer outer who goes to forest, lake or stream for health and sport, gets about ten cents' worth for a dollar of outlay. A majority will admit—to themselves at least—that after a month's vacation, they return to work with an inward consciousness of being somewhat disappointed—and beaten. We are free with our money when we have it. We are known throughout the civilized world for our lavishness in paying for our pleasures; but it humiliates us to know we have been beaten, and this is what the most of us do know at the end of a summer vacation. To the man of millions it makes little difference.

He is able to pay liberally for boats, buckboards and "body service," if he chooses to spend a summer in the North Woods. He has no need to study the questions of lightness and economy in a forest and stream outing. Let his guides take care of him; and unto them and the landlords he will give freely of his substance.

I do not write for him, and can do him little good. But there are hundreds of thousands of practical, useful men, many of them far from being rich; mechanics, artists, writers, merchants, clerks, business men—workers, so to speak—who sorely need and well deserve a season of rest and relaxation at least once a year. To these, and for these, I write.

Perhaps more than fifty years of devotion to "woodcraft" may enable me to give a few useful hints and suggestions to those whose dreams, during the close season of work, are of camp-life by flood, field and forest.

I have found that nearly all who have a real love of nature and out-of-door camp-life, spend a good deal of time and talk in planning future trips, or discussing the trips and pleasures gone by, but still dear to memory.

When the mountain streams are frozen and the Nor'land
    winds are out;

when the winter winds are drifting the bitter sleet and snow; when winter rains are making out-of-door life unendurable; when season, weather and law, combine to make it "close time" for beast, bird and man, it is well that a few congenial spirits should, at some favorite trysting place, gather around the glowing stove and exchange yarns, opinions and experiences. Perhaps no two will exactly agree on the best ground for an outing, on the flies, rods, reels, guns, etc., or half a dozen other points that may be discussed. But one thing all admit. Each and every one has gone to his chosen ground with too much impedimenta, too much duffle;* and nearly all have used boats at least twice as heavy as they need to have been. The temptation to buy this or that bit of indispensable camp-kit has been too strong, and we have gone to the blessed woods, handicapped with a load fit for a pack-mule. This is not how to do it.

Go light; the lighter the better, so that you have the simplest *materiel* for health, comfort and enjoy‧ment.

Of course, if you intend to have a permanent camp, and can reach it by boat or wagon, lightness is not so important, though even in that case it is well to guard against taking in a lot of stuff that is likely to prove of more weight than worth—only to leave it behind when you come out.

As to clothing for the woods, a good deal of non-sense has been written about "strong, coarse woolen clothes." You do not want coarse woolen clothes. Fine woolen cassimere of medium thickness for coat, vest and pantaloons, with no cotton lining. Color, slate gray or dead-leaf (either is good). Two soft, thick woolen shirts; two pairs of fine, but substantial,

---

* *Duffle.* A kind of coarse woolen cloth having a thick nap or frieze.
  Duffel. Loose material,—*Worcester.*   [—*Webster.*

woolen drawers; two pairs of strong woolen socks or
stockings; these are what you need, and all you need
in the way of clothing for the woods, excepting hat
and boots, or gaiters.   Boots are best—providing you
do not let yourself be inveigled into wearing a pair of
long-legged heavy boots with thick soles, as has been
often advised by writers who knew no better.   Heavy,
long-legged boots are a weary, tiresome incumbrance
on a hard tramp through rough woods.   Even moccasins are better.   Gaiters, all sorts of high shoes
in fact, are too bothersome about fastening and
unfastening.   Light boots are best.   Not thin,
unserviceable affairs, but light as to actual weight.
The following hints will give an idea of the best foot-
gear for the woods: Let them be single soled, single
backs and single fronts, except light, short foot-linings.
Backs of solid "country kip;" fronts of substantial
French calf; heel one inch high, with steel nails;
countered outside; straps narrow, of fine French calf
put on "astraddle," and set down to the top of the
back.   The out-sole stout, Spanish oak, and pegged
rather than sewed, although either is good.   They
will weigh considerably less than half as much as the
clumsy, costly boots usually recommended for the
woods; and the added comfort must be tested to be
understood.

The hat should be fine, soft felt, with moderately
low crown and wide brim; color to match the clothing.

The proper covering for head and feet is no slight
affair, and will be found worth some attention.   Be
careful that the boots are not too tight, or the hat too

loose. The above rig will give the tourist one shirt, one pair of drawers and pair of socks to carry as extra clothing. A soft, warm blanket-bag, open at the ends, and just long enough to cover the sleeper, with an oblong square of waterproofed cotton cloth 6x8 feet, will give warmth and shelter by night and will weigh together five or six pounds. This, with the extra clothing, will make about eight pounds of dry goods to pack over carries, which is enough. Probably, also, it will be found little enough for comfort.

During a canoe cruise across the Northern Wilderness in the summer of '83, I met many parties at different points in the woods, and the amount of unnecessary duffle with which they encumbered themselves was simply appalling. Why a shrewd business man, who goes through with a guide and makes a forest hotel his camping ground nearly every night, should handicap himself with a five-peck pack-basket full of gray woolen and gum blankets, extra clothing, pots, pans and kettles, with a 9-pound 10-bore, and two rods—yes, and an extra pair of heavy boots hanging astride of the gun—well, it is one of the things I shall never understand. My own load, including canoe, extra clothing, blanket-bag, two days' rations, pocket-axe, rod and knapsack, never exceeded 26 pounds; and I went prepared to camp out any and every night.

People who contemplate an outing in the woods are pretty apt to commence preparations a long way ahead, and to pick up many trifling articles that suggest themselves as useful and handy in camp; all well enough in their way, but making at last a too heavy load. It is better to commence by studying to ascertain just how light one can go through without especial discomfort. A good plan is to think over the trip during leisure hours, and make out a list of indispensable articles, securing them beforehand, and have them stowed in handy fashion, so that nothing needful may be missing just when and where it cannot be procured. The list will be longer than one would think, but need not be cumbersome or heavy. As I am usually credited with making a cruise or a long woods tramp with exceptionally light duffle, I will give a list of the articles I take along—going on foot over carries or through the woods.

CHAPTER II.

KNAPSACK, HATCHET, KNIVES, TINWARE, RODS, FISH-
ING TACKLE, DITTY-BAG.

THE clothing, blanket-bag and shelter-cloth are all that need be described in that line.

The next articles that I look after are knapsack (or pack basket), rod with reel, lines, flies, hooks, and all my fishing gear, pocket-axe, knives and tinware.

Firstly, the knapsack; as you are apt to carry it a great many miles, it is well to have it right, and easy-fitting at the start. Don't be induced to carry a pack basket. I am aware that it is in high favor all through the Northern Wilderness, and is also much used in many other localities where guides and sportsmen most do congregate. But I do not like it. I admit that it will carry a loaf of bread, with tea, sugar, etc., without jamming; that bottles, crockery, and other fragile duffle is safer from breakage than in an oil-cloth knapsack. But it is by no means waterproof in a rain or a splashing head sea, is more than twice as heavy—always growing heavier as it gets wetter—and I had rather have bread, tea, sugar etc., a little jammed than water-soaked. Also, it may be remarked that man is a vertebrate animal and ought to respect

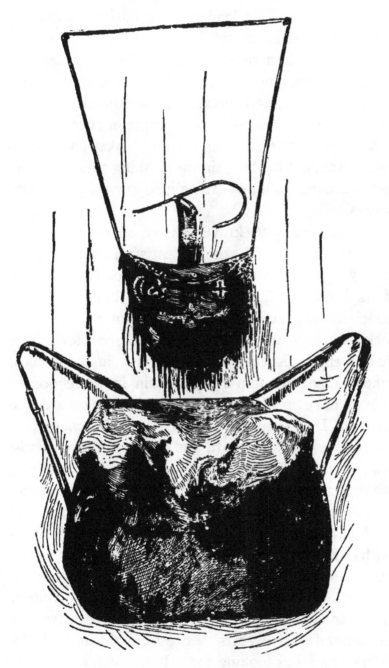

KNAPSACK AND DITTY-BAG.

his backbone. The loaded pack basket on a heavy carry never fails to get in on the most vulnerable knob of the human vertebræ. The knapsack sits easy, and does not chafe. The one shown in the engraving is of good form; and the original—which I have carried for years—is satisfactory in every respect. It holds over half a bushel, carries blanket-bag, shelter tent, hatchet, ditty-bag, tinware, fishing tackle, clothes and two days' rations. It weighs, empty, just twelve ounces.

The hatchet and knives shown in the engraving will be found to fill the bill satisfactorily so far as cutlery may be required. Each is good and useful of its kind, the hatchet especially, being the best model I have ever found for a "double-barreled" pocket-axe. And just here let me digress for a little chat on the indispensable hatchet; for it is the most difficult piece of camp kit to obtain in perfection of which I have any knowledge. Before I was a dozen years old I came to realize that a light hatchet was a *sine qua non* in woodcraft, and I also found it a most difficult thing to get. I tried shingling hatchets, lathing hatchets, and the small hatchets to be found in country hardware stores, but none of them were satisfactory. I had quite a number made by black-smiths who professed skill in making edge tools, and these were the worst of all, being like nothing on the earth or under it—murderous-looking, clumsy, and all too heavy, with no balance or proportion. I had hunted twelve years before I caught up with the pocket-axe I was looking for. It was made in Rochester, by a surgical instrument maker named Bushnell. It cost time and money to get it. I worked one rainy Sunday fashioning the pattern in wood. Spoiled a day going to Rochester, waited a day for the blade,

HATCHET AND KNIVES.

paid $3.00 for it, and lost a day coming home. Boat fare $1.00, and expenses $2.00, besides three days lost time, with another rainy Sunday for making leather sheath and hickory handle.

My witty friends, always willing to help me out in

figuring the cost of my hunting and fishing gear, made the following business-like estimate, which they placed where I would be certain to see it the first thing in the morning. Premising that of the five who assisted in that little joke, all stronger, bigger fellows than myself, four have gone "where they never see the sun," I will copy the statement as it stands to-day, on paper yellow with age. For I have kept it over forty years.

Aug. 15, 1843.

DR.

To getting up one limber-go-shiftless pocket-axe:

Cost of blade............................	$3 00
Fare on boat.............................	1 00
Expenses for 3 days.....................	3 00
Three days lost time at $1.25 per day......	3 75
Two days making model, handle and sheath, say.	2 00
Total................................	$12 75
Per contra, by actual value of axe...........	2 00
Balance..............................	$10 75

Then they raised a horse laugh, and the cost of that hatchet became a standing joke and a slur on my "business ability." What aggravated me most was, that the rascals were not so far out in their calculation. And was I so far wrong? That hatchet was my favorite for nearly thirty years. It has been "upset" twice by skilled workmen; and, if my friend "Bero" has not lost it, is still in service.

Would I have gone without it any year for one or two dollars? But I prefer the double blade. I want one thick, stunt edge for knots, deer's bones, etc., and a fine, keen edge for cutting clear timber.

A word as to knife, or knives. These are of prime necessity, and should be of the best, both as to shape and temper. The "bowies" and "hunting knives" usually kept on sale, are thick, clumsy affairs, with a sort of ridge along the middle of the blade, murderous looking, but of little use; rather fitted to adorn a dime novel or the belt of "Billy the Kid," than the outfit of the hunter. The one shown in the cut is thin in the blade, and handy for skinning, cutting meat, or eating with. The strong double-bladed pocket knife is the best model I have yet found, and, in connection with the sheath knife, is all sufficient for camp use. It is not necessary to take table cutlery into the woods. A good fork may be improvised from a beech or birch stick; and the half of a fresh-water mussel shell, with a split stick by way of handle, makes an excellent spoon.

My entire outfit for cooking and eating dishes comprises five pieces of tinware. This is when stopping in a permanent camp. When cruising and tramping, I take just two pieces in the knapsack.

I get a skillful tinsmith to make one dish as follows: Six inches on bottom, 6¾ inches on top, side 2 inches high. The bottom is of the heaviest tin procurable, the sides of lighter tin, and seamed to be water-tight without solder. The top simply turned, without wire. The second dish to be made the same, but small enough to nest in the first, and also to fit into it when inverted as a cover. Two other dishes made from common pressed tinware, with the tops cut off and turned, also without wire. They are fitted so that they all nest, taking no more room than the largest dish alone, and each of the three smaller dishes makes a perfect cover for the next larger. The other piece is a tin camp-kettle, also of the heaviest tin, and seamed water-tight. It holds two quarts, and the other dishes nest in it perfectly, so that when packed the whole take just as much room as the kettle alone. I should mention that the strong ears are set below the rim of the kettle, and the bale falls outside, so, as none of the dishes have any handle, there are no aggravating "stickouts" to wear and abrade. The snug affair weighs, all told, two pounds. I have met parties in the North Woods whose one frying pan weighed more—with its handle three feet long. How ever did they get through the brush with such a culinary terror?

It is only when I go into a very accessible camp that I take so much as five pieces of tinware along. I once made a ten days' tramp through an unbroken wilderness on foot, and all the dish I took was a ten-cent tin; it was enough. I believe I will tell the story of that tramp before I get through. For I saw more game in the ten days than I ever saw before or since in a season; and I am told that the whole region is now a thrifty farming country, with the deer nearly all gone. They were plenty enough thirty-nine years ago this very month.

I feel more diffidence in speaking of rods than of any other matter connected with out-door sports. The number and variety of rods and makers; the enthusiasm of trout and fly "cranks;" the fact that

angling does not take precedence of all other sports
with me, with the humiliating confession that I am
not above worms and sinkers, or minnow-tails and
white grubs—this and these constrain me to be brief.

But, as I have been a fisher all my life, from my pin-
hook days to the present time; as I have run the list
pretty well up, from brook minnows to 100-pound
albacores, I may be pardoned for a few remarks on
the rod and the use thereof.

A rod may be a very high-toned, high-priced,
æsthetic plaything, costing $50 to $75, or it may be
—a rod. A plain, useful, business rod; in which
case it is not wise to lay out more than $5 to $10 on
it. By all means let the man of money indulge his
fancy for a costly split bamboo. He might do worse.
But the plain common-sense sportsman will find a
well-made lancewood, of from 8 to 10 ounces,
sufficient. I have used a 4½-ounce rod and found it
large enough and strong enough for brook trout; but,
as I never add a second rod to my kit, I prefer the
one to weigh not less than eight ounces; ten is better.
I handled, last summer, a 10-ounce rod made by
Cruttenden of Cazenovia, N. Y., and costing only
$5.75. It was satisfactory in every respect; and I
could see no special superiority in a split bamboo
costing $25, which one of my friends sported.
Charles Dudley Warner, who writes charmingly of
woods life, has the following in regard to trout fishing,
which is so neatly humorous that it will bear repeating:

"It is well known that no person who regards his
reputation will ever kill a trout with anything but a

fly. It requires some training on the part of the trout to take to this method. The uncultivated trout in unfrequented waters prefers the bait; and the rural people, whose sole object in going a-fishing appears to be to catch fish, indulge them in their primitive taste for the worm. No sportsman, however, will use anything but a fly—except he happens to be alone." Speaking of rods, he says: "The rod is a bamboo weighing seven ounces, which has to be spliced with a winding of silk thread every time it is used. This is a tedious process; but, by fastening the joints in this way, a uniform spring is secured in the rod. No one devoted to high art would think of using a socket joint."

In the summer of '83, during a seven weeks' tour in the Northern Wilderness, my only rod was a bethabara Henshall. It came to hand with two bait-tips only; but I added a lancewood fly-tip, and it made an excellent "general fishing rod." With it I could handle a large bass or pickerel; it was a capital bait-rod for brook trout; as a fly-rod it has pleased me well enough. It is likely to go with me again. But it is not yet decided which is best, and I leave every man his own opinion. Only, I think one rod enough.

And don't neglect to take what sailors call a "ditty-bag." This may be a little sack of chamois leather about 4 inches wide by 6 inches in length. Mine is before me as I write. Emptying the contents, I find it inventories as follows: A dozen hooks, running in size from small minnow hooks to large Limericks; four lines of six yards each, varying from the finest to a size sufficient for a ten-pound fish; three darning needles and a few common sewing needles; a dozen buttons; sewing silk; thread, and a small ball of strong yarn for darning socks; sticking salve; a bit of shoe-maker's wax; beeswax; sinkers, and a very fine file for sharpening hooks. The ditty-bag weighs, with contents, 2½ ounces; and it goes in a small buckskin bullet pouch, which I wear almost as constantly as my hat. The pouch has a sheath strongly sewed on the back side of it, where the light hunting knife is always at hand, and it also carries a two-ounce vial of fly medicine, a vial of "pain killer," and two or three gangs of hooks on brass wire snells—of which, more in another place. I can always go down into that pouch for a water-proof match safe, strings, com-pass, bits of linen and scarlet flannel (for frogging), copper tacks, and other light duffle. It is about as handy a piece of woods-kit as I carry.

I hope no æsthetic devotee of the fly-rod will lay down the book in disgust when I confess to a weakness for frogging. I admit that it is not high-toned sport; and yet I have got a good deal of amusement out of it. The persistence with which a large batrachian will snap at a bit of red flannel after being several times hooked on the same lure, and the comical way in which he will scuttle off with a quick succession of short jumps after each release; the cheerful manner in which, after each bout, he will tune up his deep, bass pipe—ready for another greedy snap at an ibis fly or red rag—is rather funny. And his hind legs; rolled in meal and nicely browned, are preferable to trout or venison.

CHAPTER III.

GETTING LOST.—CAMPING OUT.—ROUGHING IT OR
SMOOTHING IT.—INSECTS.—CAMPS, AND
HOW TO MAKE THEM.

WITH a large majority of prospective tourists and outers, "camping out" is a leading factor in the summer vacation. And during the long winter months they are prone to collect in little knots and talk much of camps, fishing, hunting, and "roughing it." The last phrase is very popular and always cropping out in the talks on matters pertaining to a vacation in the woods. I dislike the phrase. We do not go to the green woods and crystal waters to rough it, we go to smooth it. We get it rough enough at home; in towns and cities; in shops, offices, stores, banks—anywhere that we may be placed—with the necessity always present of being on time and up to our work; of providing for dependent ones; of keeping up, catching up, or getting left. "Alas for the life-long battle, whose bravest slogan is bread."

As for the few fortunate ones who have no call to take a hand in any strife or struggle, who not only have all the time there is, but a great deal that they cannot dispose of with any satisfaction to themselves or anybody else—I am not writing for them; but only to those of the world's workers who go, or would like to go, every summer to the woods. And to these I would say, don't rough it; make it as smooth, as restful and pleasurable as you can.

To this end you need pleasant days and peaceful nights. You cannot afford to be tormented and poisoned by insects, nor kept awake at night by cold and damp, nor to exhaust your strength by hard tramps and heavy loads. Take it easy, and always keep cool. Nine men out of ten, on finding themselves lost in the woods, fly into a panic, and quarrel with the compass. Never do that. The compass is always right, or nearly so. It is not many years since an able-bodied man—sportsman of course—lost his way in the North Woods, and took fright, as might be expected. He was well armed and well found for a week in the woods. What ought to have been only an interesting adventure, became a tragedy. He tore through thickets and swamps in his senseless panic, until he dropped and died through fright, hunger and exhaustion.

A well authenticated story is told of a guide in the Oswegatchie region, who perished in the same way. Guides are not infallible; I have known more than one to get lost. Wherefore, should you be tramping through a pathless forest on a cloudy day, and should the sun suddenly break from under a cloud in the northwest about noon, don't be scared. The last day is not at hand, and the planets have not become

mixed; only, you are turned. You have gradually swung around, until you are facing northwest when you meant to travel south. It has a mud-
dling effect on the mind—this getting lost in the
woods. But, if you can collect and arrange your
gray brain matter, and suppress all panicky feeling,
it is easily got along with. For instance; it is
morally certain that you commenced swinging to
southwest, then west, to northwest. Had you kept
on until you were heading directly north, you could
rectify your course simply by following a true south
course. But, as you have varied three-eighths of the
circle, set your compass and travel by it to the
southeast, until, in your judgment, you have about
made up the deviation; then go straight south,
and you will not be far wrong. Carry the compass
in your hand and look at it every few minutes; for
the tendency to swerve from a straight course when
a man is once lost—and nearly always to the right—
is a thing past understanding.

As regards poisonous insects, it may be said that,
to the man with clean, bleached, tender skin, they
are, at the start, an unendurable torment. No one
can enjoy life with a smarting, burning, swollen face,
while the attacks on every exposed inch of skin are
persistent and constant. I have seen a young man
after two days' exposure to these pests come out of
the woods with one eye entirely closed and the brow
hanging over it like a clam shell, while face and
hands were almost hideous from inflammation and
puffiness. The St. Regis and St. Francis Indians,

although born and reared in the woods, by no means make light of the black fly.

It took the man who could shoot Phantom Falls to find out, "Its bite is not severe, nor is it ordinarily poisonous. There may be an occasional exception to this rule; but beside the bite of the mosquito, it is comparatively mild and harmless." And again: 'Gnats * * * in my way of thinking, are much worse than the black fly or mosquito." So says Murray. Our observations differ. A thousand mosquitoes and as many gnats can bite me without leaving a mark, or having any effect save the pain of the bite while they are at work. But each bite of the black fly makes a separate and distinct boil, that will not heal and be well in two months.

While fishing for brook trout in July last, I ran into a swarm of them on Moose River, and got badly bitten. I had carelessly left my fly medicine behind. On the first of October the bites had not ceased to be painful, and it was three months before they disappeared entirely. Frank Forester says, in his "Fish and Fishing," page 371, that he has never fished for the red-fleshed trout of Hamilton county, "being deterred therefrom by dread of that curse of the summer angler, the black fly, which is to me especially venomous."

"Adirondack Murray" gives extended directions for beating these little pests by the use of buckskin gloves with chamois gauntlets, Swiss mull, fine muslin, etc. Then he advises a mixture of sweet oil and tar, which is to be applied to face and hands; and he adds that it is easily washed off, leaving the skin soft and smooth as an infant's; all of which is true. But, more than forty years' experience in the woods has taught me that the following receipt is infallibly anywhere that *sancudos, moquims*, or our own poisonous insects do most abound.

It was published in *Forest and Stream* in the summer of 1880, and again in '83. I has been pretty widely quoted and adopted, and I have never known it to fail: Three ounces pine tar, two ounces castor oil, one ounce pennyroyal oil. Simmer all together over a slow fire, and bottle for use. You will hardly need more than a two-ounce vial full in a season. One ounce has lasted me six weeks in the woods. Rub it in thoroughly and liberally at first, and after you have established a good glaze, a little replenishing from day to day will be sufficient. And don't fool with soap and towels where insects are plenty. A good safe coat of this varnish grows better the longer it is kept on—and it is cleanly and wholesome. If you get your face or hands crocky or smutty about the camp-fire, wet the corner of your handkerchief and rub it off, not forgetting to apply the varnish at once, wherever you have cleaned it off. Last summer I carried a cake of soap and a towel in my knapsack through the North Woods for a seven weeks' tour, and never used either a single time. When I had established a good glaze on the skin, it was too valuable to be sacrificed for any weak whim connected with soap and water. When I struck a woodland hotel, I found soap and towels plenty enough.

I found the mixture gave one's face the ruddy tanned look supposed to be indicative of health and hard muscle. A thorough ablution in the public wash basin reduced the color, but left the skin very soft and smooth; in fact, as a lotion for the skin it is excellent. It is a soothing and healing application for poisonous bites already received.

I have given some space to the insect question, but no more than it deserves or requires. The venomous little wretches are quite important enough to spoil many a well planned trip to the woods, and it is best to beat them from the start. You will find that immunity from insects and a comfortable camp are the two first and most indispensable requisites of an outing in the woods. And just here I will briefly tell how a young friend of mine went to the woods, some twenty-five years ago. He was a bank clerk, and a good fellow withal, with a leaning toward camp-life.

For months, whenever we met, he would introduce his favorite topics, fishing, camping out, etc. At last in the hottest of the hot months, the time came. He put in an appearance with a fighting cut on his hair, a little stiff straw hat, and a soft skin, bleached by long confinement in a close office. I thought he looked a little tender; but he was sanguine. He could rough it, could sleep on the bare ground with the root of a tree for a pillow; as for mosquitoes and punkies, he never minded them.

We went in a party of five—two old hunters and three youngsters, the latter all enthusiasm and pluck

—at first. Toward the last end of a heavy eight-mile tramp, they grew silent, and slapped and scratched nervously. Arriving at the camping spot, they worked fairly well, but were evidently weakening a little. By the time we were ready to turn in they were reduced pretty well to silence and suffering —especially the bank clerk, Jean L. The punkies were eager for his tender skin, and they were rank poison to him. He muffled his head in a blanket and tried to sleep, but it was only a partial success. When, by suffocating himself, he obtained a little relief from insect bites, there were stubs and knotty roots continually poking themselves among his ribs, or digging into his backbone.

I have often had occasion to observe that stubs, roots and small stones, etc., have a perverse tendency to abrade the economy of people unused to the woods. Mr. C. D. Warner has noticed the same thing, I believe.

On the whole, Jean and the other youngsters behaved very well. Although they turned out in the morning with red, swollen faces and half closed eyes, they all went trouting and caught about 150 small trout between them. They did their level bravest to make a jolly thing of it; but Jean's attempt to watch a deerlick, resulted in a wetting through the sudden advent of a shower; and the shower drove about all the punkies and mosquitoes in the neighborhood under our roof for shelter. I never saw them more plenty or worse. Jean gave in, and varnished his pelt thoroughly with my "punkie dope," as he called it; but, too late; the mischief was done. And the second trial was worse to those youngsters than the first. More insects. More stubs and knots. Owing to these little annoyances, they arrived at home several days before their friends expected them— leaving enough rations in camp to last Old Sile and the writer a full week. And the moral of it is, if they had fitted themselves for the woods before going there, the trip would have been a pleasure instead of a misery.

One other little annoyance I will mention, as a common occurrence among those who camp out; this is the lack of a pillow. I suppose I have camped fifty times with people, who, on turning in, were squirming around for a long time, trying to get a rest for the head. Boots are the most common resort. But, when you place a boot-leg—or two of them—under your head, they collapse, and make a head-rest less than half an inch thick. Just why it never occurs to people that a stuffing of moss, leaves, or hemlock browse, would fill out the boot-legs and make a passable pillow, is another conundrum I can- not answer. But, there is another and better way of making a pillow for camp use, which I will describe further on.

And now I wish to devote some space to one of the most important adjuncts of woodcraft, *i. e.*, camps; how to make them, and how to make them com- fortable. There are camps, and camps. There are camps in the North Woods that are really fine villas, costing thousands of dollars, and there are log-houses, and shanties, and bark camps, and A tents, and walled tents, shelter tents and shanty tents. But, I assume that the camp best fitted to the wants of the average outer is the one that combines the essentials of dryness, lightness, portability, cheapness, and is easily and quickly put up. Another essential is, that it must admit of a bright fire in front by night or day. I will give short descriptions of the forest shelters (camps) I have found handiest and most useful:

Firstly, I will mention a sort of camp that was described in a sportsman's paper, and has since been largely quoted and used. It is made by fastening a horizontal pole to a couple of contiguous trees, and then putting on a heavy covering of hemlock boughs, shingling them with the tips downward, of course. A fire is to be made at the roots of one of the trees. This, with plenty of boughs, may be made to stand a pretty stiff rain; but it is only a damp arbor, and no camp, properly speaking. A forest camp should always admit of a bright fire in front, with a lean-to or shed roof overhead, to reflect the fire heat on the bedding below. Any camp that falls short of this, lacks the requirements of warmth, brightness and healthfulness. This is why I discard all close, canvas tents.

The simplest and most primitive of all camps is the "Indian camp." It is easily and quickly made; is warm and comfortable, and stands a pretty heavy rain when properly put up. This is how it is made: Let us say you are out and have slightly missed your way. The coming gloom warns you that night is shutting down. You are no tenderfoot. You know that a place of rest is essential to health and comfort

INDIAN CAMP.

through the long, cold, November night. You dive down the first little hollow until you strike a rill of water, for water is a prime necessity. As you draw, your hatchet you take in the whole situation at a glance. The little stream is gurgling downward in a half choked frozen way. There is a huge soddened hemlock lying across it. One clip of the hatchet shows it will peel. There is plenty of smaller timber standing around; long, slim poles, with a tuft of foliage on top. Five minutes suffices to drop one of these, cut a twelve-foot pole from it, sharpen the pole at each end, jam one end into the ground and the other into the rough bark of a scraggy hemlock, and there is your ridge-pole. Now go—with your hatchet —for the bushiest and most promising young hemlocks within reach. Drop them and draw them to camp rapidly. Next, you need a fire. There are fifty hard, resinous limbs sticking up from the prone hemlock; lop off a few of these, and split the largest into match timber; reduce the splinters to shavings, scrape the wet leaves from your prospective fire-place, and strike a match on the balloon part of your trousers. If you are a woodsman you will strike but one. Feed the fire slowly at first; it will gain fast. When you have a blaze ten feet high, look at your watch. It is 6 P. M. You don't want to turn in before 10 o'clock, and you have four hours to kill before bed-time. Now, tackle the old hemlock; take off every dry limb, and then peel the bark and bring it to camp. You will find this takes an hour or more.

Next, strip every limb from your young hemlocks, and shingle them on to your ridge-pole. This will make a sort of bear den, very well calculated to give you a comfortable night's rest. The bright fire will

soon dry the ground that is to be your bed, and you
will have plenty of time to drop another small hemlock and make a bed of browse a foot thick. You do
it. Then you make your pillow. Now, this pillow is
essential to comfort, and very simple. It is half a
yard of muslin, sewed up as a bag, and filled with
moss or hemlock browse. You can empty it and put
it in your pocket, where it takes up about as much
room as a handkerchief. You have other little muslin bags—an' you be wise. One holds a couple of
ounces of good tea; another, sugar; another is kept to
put your loose duffle in; money, match safe, pocket-
knife. You have a pat of butter and a bit of pork,
with a liberal slice of brown bread; and before
turning in you make a cup of tea, broil a slice of
pork, and indulge in a lunch.

Ten o'clock comes. The time has not passed
tediously. You are warm, dry and well-fed. Your
old friends, the owls, come near the fire-light and
salute you with their strange wild notes; a distant
fox sets up for himself with his odd, barking cry,
and you turn in. Not ready to sleep just yet.

But you drop off; and it is two bells in the morning watch when you waken with a sense of chill and
darkness. The fire has burned low, and snow is
falling. The owls have left, and a deep silence broods
over the cold, still forest. You rouse the fire, and,
as the bright light shines to the furthest recesses of
your forest den, get out the little pipe, and reduce a
bit of navy plug to its lowest denomination. The
smoke curls lazily upward; the fire makes you warm

and drowsy, and again you lie down—to again
awaken with a sense of chilliness—to find the fire
burned low, and daylight breaking.   You have slept
better than you would in your own room at home.
You have slept in an "Indian camp."

You have also learned the difference between such
a simple shelter and an open air *bivouac* under a tree
or beside an old log.

Another easily made and very comfortable camp is
the "brush shanty," as it is usually called in Northern
Pennsylvania.   The frame for such a shanty is a cross-
pole resting on two crotches about six feet high, and
enough straight poles to make a foundation for the
thatch.   The poles are laid about six inches apart,
one end on the ground, the other on the crosspole,
and at a pretty sharp angle.   The thatch is made of
the fan-like boughs cut from a thrifty young hemlock,
and are to be laid bottom upward and feather end
down.   Commence to lay them from the ground, and
work up to the crosspole, shingling them carefully as
you go.   If the thatch be laid a foot in thickness, and
well done, the shanty will stand a pretty heavy rain
—better than the average bark roof, which is only
rain-proof in dry weather.

A bark camp, however, may be a very neat sylvan
affair, provided you are camping where spruce or
balsam fir may be easily reached, and in the hot
months when bark will "peel"; and you have a day
in which to work at a camp.   The best bark camps
I have ever seen are in the Adirondacks.   Some of
them are rather elaborate in construction, requiring

two or more days' hard labor by a couple of guides. When the stay is to be a long one, and the camp permanent, perhaps it will pay.

As good a camp as I have ever tried—perhaps the best—is the "shanty-tent," shown in the illustration. It is easily put up, is comfortable, neat, and absolutely rain-proof. Of course, it may be of any required size; but, for a party of two, the following dimensions and directions will be found all sufficient:

Firstly, the roof. This is merely a sheet of strong cotton cloth 9 feet long by 4 or 4½ feet in width. The sides, of the same material, to be 4½ feet deep at front, and 2 feet deep at the back. This gives 7 feet along the edge of the roof, leaving 2 feet for turning down at the back end of the shanty. It will be seen that the sides must be "cut bias," to compensate for the angle of the roof, otherwise the shanty will not be square and ship-shape when put up. Allowing for waste in cutting, it takes nearly 3 yards of cloth for each side. The only labor required in making, is to cut the sides to the proper shape, and stitch them to the roof. No buttons, strings or loops. The cloth does not even require hemming. It does, however, need a little water-proofing; for which the following receipt will answer very well, and add little or nothing to the weight: To 10 quarts of water add 10 ounces of lime, and 4 ounces of alum; let it stand until clear; fold the cloth snugly and put it in another vessel, pour the solution on it, let it soak for 12 hours; then rinse in luke-warm rain water, stretch and dry in the sun, and the shanty-tent is ready for use.

To put it up properly, make a neat frame as follows: Two strong stakes or posts for the front, driven firmly in the ground 4½ feet apart; at a distance of 6 feet 10 inches from these, drive two other posts—these to be 4 feet apart—for back end of shanty. The front posts to be 4½ feet high, the back posts only 2 feet. The former, also to incline a little toward each other above, so as to measure from outside of posts, just 4 feet at top. This gives a little more width at front end of shanty, adding space and warmth. No crotches are used in putting up the shanty-tent. Each of the four posts are fitted on the top to receive a flat-ended cross-pole, and admit of nailing. When the posts are squarely ranged and driven, select two straight, hard-wood rods, 2 inches in diameter, and 7 feet in length—or a little more. Flatten the ends carefully and truly, lay them alongside on top from post to post, and fasten them with a light nail at each end. Now, select two more straight rods of the same size, but a little over 4 feet in length; flatten the ends of these as you did the others, lay them crosswise from side to side, and lapping the ends of the other rods; fasten them solidly by driving a sixpenny nail through the ends and into the posts, and you have a square frame 7x4 feet. But it is not yet complete. Three light rods are needed for rafters. These are to be placed lengthwise of the roof at equal distances apart, and nailed or tied to keep them in place. Then take two straight poles a little over 7 feet long, and some 3 inches in diameter. These are to be accurately flattened at the ends, and nailed to the bottom of the posts, snug to the ground, on outside of posts. A foot-log and head-log are indispensable. These should be about 5 inches in diameter, and of a length to just reach from outside to outside of posts. They should be squared at ends, and the foot-log placed against the front post, outside, and held firmly in place by two wooden pins. The head-log is fastened the same way, except that it goes against the inside of the back posts; and the frame is complete. Round off all sharp angles or corners with knife and hatchet, and proceed to spread and fasten the cloth. Lay the roof on evenly, and tack it truly to the front cross-rod, using about a dozen six-ounce tacks. Stretch the cloth to its bearings, and tack it at the back end in the same manner. Stretch it sidewise and tack the sides to the side poles, fore and aft. Tack front and back ends of sides to the front and back posts. Bring down the 2-foot flap of roof at back end of shanty; stretch, and tack it snugly to the back posts—and your sylvan house is done. It is rain-proof, wind-proof, warm and comfortable. The foot and head logs define the limits of your forest dwelling; within which you may pile fragrant hemlock browse as thick as you please, and renew it from day to day. It is the perfect camp.

You may put it up with less care and labor, and make it do very well. But, I have tried to explain how to do it in the best manner; to make it all sufficient for an entire season. And it takes longer to tell it on paper than to do it.

When I go to the woods with a partner, and we

arrive at our camping ground, I like him to get his fishing rig together, and start out for a half day's exercise with his favorite flies, leaving me to make the camp according to my own notions of woodcraft. If he will come back about dusk with a few pounds of trout, I will have a pleasant camp and a bright fire for him. And if he has enjoyed wading an icy stream more than I have making the camp—he has had a good day.

Perhaps it may not be out of place to say that the camp, made as above, calls for fifteen bits of timber, posts, rods, etc., a few shingle nails, and some six-penny wrought nails, with a paper of six-ounce tacks. Nails and tacks will weigh about five ounces, and are always useful. In tacking the cloth, turn the raw edge in until you have four thicknesses, as a single thickness is apt to tear. If you desire to strike camp, it takes about ten minutes to draw and save all the nails and tacks, fold the cloth smoothly, and deposit the whole in your knapsack. If you wish to get up a shelter tent on fifteen minutes' notice, cut and sharpen a twelve-foot pole as for the Indian camp, stick one end in the ground, the other in the rough bark of a large tree—hemlock is best—hang the cloth on the pole, fasten the sides to rods, and the rods to the ground with inverted crotches, and your shelter tent is ready for you to creep under.

The above description of the shanty-tent may seem a trifle elaborate, but I hope it is plain. The affair weighs just three pounds, and it takes a skillful woods-man about three hours of easy work to put it in the

shape described. Leaving out some of the work, and
only aiming to get it up in square shape as quickly
as possible, I can put it up in an hour. The shanty

SHANTY-TENT AND CAMP-FIRE.

as it should be, is shown in the illustration very fairly.
And the shape of the cloth when spread out, is shown
in the diagram on page 37. On the whole, it is the
best form of close-sided tent I have found. It admits

of a bright fire in front, without which a forest camp is just no camp at all to me. I have suffered enough in close, dark, cheerless, damp tents.

More than thirty years ago I became disgusted with the clumsy, awkward, comfortless affairs that, under many different forms, went under the name of camps. Gradually I came to make a study of "camping out." It would take too much time and space, should I undertake to describe all the different styles and forms I have tried. But, I will mention a few of the best and worst.

The old Down East "coal cabin" embodied the principle of the Indian camp. The frame was simply two strong crotches set firmly in the ground at a distance of eight feet apart, and interlocking at top. These supported a stiff ridge-pole fifteen feet long, the small end sharpened and set in the ground. Refuse boards, shooks, stakes, etc., were placed thickly from the ridge-pole to the ground; a thick layer of straw was laid over these, and the whole was covered a foot thick with earth and sods, well beaten down. A stone wall five feet high at back and sides made a most excellent fire-place; and these cabins were weather-proof and warm, even in zero weather. But, they were too cumbersome, and included too much labor for the ordinary hunter and angler. Also, they were open to the objection, that while wide enough in front, they ran down to a dismal, cold peak at the far end. Remembering, however, the many pleasant winter nights I had passed with the coal-burners, I bought a supply of oil-cloth and rigged it on the same principle. It was a partial success, and I used it for one season. But that cold, peaked, dark space was always back of my head, and it seemed like an iceberg. It was in vain that I tied a handkerchief about my head, or drew a stocking-leg over it. That miserable, icy angle was always there. And it would only shelter one man anyhow. When winter drove me out of the woods I gave it to an enthusiastic young friend,

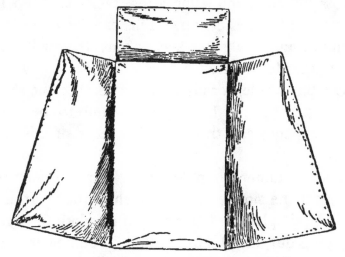

SHANTY-TENT SPREAD OUT.

bought some more oil-cloth, and commenced a shanty-tent that was meant to be perfect. A good many leisure hours were spent in cutting and sewing that shanty, which proved rather a success. It afforded a perfect shelter for a space 7x4 feet, but was a trifle heavy to pack, and the glazing began to crack and peel off in a short time. I made another and larger one of stout drilling, soaked in lime-water and alum; and this was all that could be asked when put up properly on a frame. But, the sides and ends being sewed to the roof made it unhandy to use as a shelter, when shelter was needed on short notice. So I ripped the back ends of the sides loose from the flap, leaving it, when spread out, as shown in the diagram. This was better; when it was necessary to make some sort of shelter in short order, it could be done with a single pole as used in the Indian camp, laying the tent across the pole, and using a few tacks to keep it in place at sides and center. This can be done in ten minutes, and makes a shelter-tent that will turn a heavy rain for hours.

On the whole, for all kinds of weather, the shanty-tent is perhaps the best style of camp to be had at equal expense and trouble. The cost of it is about $1.25.

For a summer camp, however, I have finally come to prefer the simple lean-to or shed roof. It is the lightest, simplest and cheapest of all cloth devices for camping out, and I have found it sufficient for all weathers from June until the fall of the leaves. It is only a sheet of strong cotton cloth 9x7 feet, and soaked in lime and alum-water as the other. The only labor in making it is sewing two breadths of sheeting together. It needs no hemming, binding, loops or buttons, but is to be stretched on a frame as described for the brush shanty, and held in place with tacks. The one I have used for two seasons cost sixty cents, and weighs 2¼ pounds. It makes a good shelter for a party of three; and if it be found a little too breezy for cool nights, a sufficient windbreak can be made by driving light stakes at the sides and weaving in a siding of hemlock boughs.

Lastly, whatever cloth structure you may erect to use for a camp, do not fail to cover the roof with a screen of green boughs before building your camp-fire. Because, there will usually be one fellow in camp who has a penchant for feeding the fire with old mulchy deadwood and brush, for the fun of watching the blaze, and the sparks that are prone to fly upward; forgetting that the blazing cinders are also prone to drop downward on the roof of the tent, burning holes in it.

I have spoken of some of the best camps I know. The worst ones are the A and wall tents, with all closed camps in which one is required to seclude himself through the hours of sleep in damp and darkness, utterly cut off from the cheerful, healthful light and warmth of the camp-fire.

CHAPTER IV.

HARDLY second in importance to a warm, dry camp, is the camp-fire. In point of fact, the warmth, dryness, and healthfulness of a forest camp are mainly dependent on the way the fire is managed and kept up. No asthmatic or consumptive patient ever regained health by dwelling in a close, damp tent.

I once camped for a week in a wall tent, with a Philadelphia party, and in cold weather. We had a little sheet iron fiend, called a camp-stove. When well fed with bark, knots and chips, it would get red hot, and, heaven knows, give out heat enough. By the time we were sound asleep, it would subside; and we would presently awake with chattering teeth to kindle her up again, take a smoke and a nip, turn in for another nap—to awaken again half frozen. It was a poor substitute for the open camp and bright fire. An experience of fifty years convinces me that a large percentage of the benefit obtained by invalids from camp life is attributable to the open camp and

well-managed camp-fire. And the latter is usually
handled in a way that is too sad, too wasteful; in
short, badly botched. For instance.

It happened in the summer of '81 that I was making a canoe trip in the Northern Wilderness, and as
Raquette Lake is the largest and about the most
interesting lake in the North Woods, I spent about a
week paddling, fishing, etc. I made my headquarters
at Ed. Bennett's woodland hostelry, "Under the
Hemlocks." As the hotel was filled with men, women
and crying children, bitten to agony by punkies and
mosquitoes, I chose to spread my blanket in a well-
made bark shanty, which a sign-board in black and
white said was the "Guides' Camp."

And this camp was a very popular institution.
Here it was that every evening, when night had settled
down on forest and lake, the guests of the hotel
would gather to lounge on the bed of fresh balsam
browse, chat, sing and enjoy the huge camp-fire.

No woodland hotel will long remain popular that
does not keep up a bright, cheery, out-o'-door fire.
And the fun of it—to an old woodsman—is in noting
how like a lot of school children they all act about
the fire. Ed. Bennett had a man, a North Woods
trapper, in his employ, whose chief business was to
furnish plenty of wood for the guides' camp, and
start a good fire every evening by sundown. As it
grew dark and the blaze shone high and bright, the
guests would begin to straggle in; and every man,
woman and child seemed to view it as a religious duty
to pause by the fire, and add a stick or two, before

passing into camp. The wood was thrown on end-
wise, crosswise, or any way, so that it would burn,
precisely as a crowd of boys make a bonfire on the
village green. The object being, apparently, to get
rid of the wood in the shortest possible time.

When the fire burnt low, toward midnight, the
guests would saunter off to the hotel; and the guides,
who had been waiting impatiently, would organize
what was left of the fire, roll themselves in their
blankets, and turn in. I suggested to the trapper
that he and I make one fire as it should be, and
maybe they would follow suit—which would save
half the fuel, with a better fire. But he said, "No;
they like to build bonfires, and 'Ed.' can stand the
wood, because it is best to let them have their own
way. Time seems to hang heavy on their hands
—and they pay well." Summer boarders, tourists
and sportsmen, are not the only men who know
how to build a camp-fire all wrong.

When I first came to Northern Pennsylvania, thirty-
five years ago, I found game fairly abundant; and, as
I wanted to learn the country where deer most
abounded, I naturally cottoned to the local hunters.
Good fellows enough, and conceited, as all local
hunters and anglers are apt to be. Strong, good
hunters and axe-men, to the manor born, and prone
to look on any outsider as a tenderfoot. Their mode
of building camp-fires was a constant vexation to me.
They made it a point to always have a heavy sharp
axe in camp, and toward night some sturdy chopper
would cut eight or ten logs as heavy as the whole

party could lug to camp with hand-spikes. The size of the logs was proportioned to the muscular force in camp. If there was a party of six or eight, the logs would be twice as heavy as when we were three or four. Just at dark, there would be a log heap built in front of the camp, well chinked with bark, knots and small sticks; and, for the next two hours, one could hardly get at the fire to light a pipe. But, the fire was sure though slow. By 10 or 11 P. M. it would work its way to the front, and the camp would be warm and light. The party would turn in, and deep sleep would fall on a lot of tired hunters—for two or three hours. By which time some fellow near the middle was sure to throw his blanket off with a spiteful jerk, and dash out of camp with, "Holy Moses! I can't stand this; it's an oven."

Another Snorer (partially waking).—"N-r-r-r-m, gu-r-r-r, ugh. Can't you—deaden—fire—a little?"

First Speaker.—"Deaden h—. If you want the fire deadened, get up and help throw off some of these logs."

Another (in coldest corner of shanty).—"What's 'er matter—with a-you fellows? Better dig out—an' cool off in the snow. Shanty's comfor'ble enough."

His minority report goes unheeded. The camp is roasted out. Strong hands and hand-spikes pry a couple of glowing logs from the front and replace them with two cold, green logs; the camp cools off, and the party takes to blankets once more—to turn out again at 5 A. M., and inaugurate breakfast. The fire is not in favorable shape for culinary operations, the heat is mainly on the back side, just where it isn't wanted. The few places level enough to set a pot or pan are too hot; and, in short, where there is any fire, there is too much. One man sees, with intense disgust, the nozzle of his coffee-pot drop into the fire. He makes a rash grab to save his coffee, and gets away—with the handle, which hangs on just enough to upset the pot.

"Old Al.," who is frying a slice of pork over a bed of coals that would melt a gun barrel, starts a horse laugh, that is cut short by a blue flash and an explosion of pork fat, which nearly blinds him. And the writer, taking in these mishaps in the very spirit of fun and frolic, is suddenly sobered and silenced by seeing his venison steak drop from the end of the "frizzling stick," and disappear between two glowing logs. The party manages, however, to get off on the hunt at daylight, with full stomachs; and perhaps the hearty fun and laughter more than compensate for these little mishaps.

This is digression. But, I am led to it by the recollection of many nights spent in camps and around camp-fires, pretty much as described above. I can smile to-day at the remembrance of the calm, superior way in which the old hunters of that day would look down on me, as from the upper branches of a tall hemlock, when I ventured to suggest that a better fire could be made with half the fuel and less than half the labor. They would kindly remark, "Oh, you are a Boston boy. You are used to paying $8.00 a cord for wood. We have no call to save

wood here. We can afford to burn it by the acre."
Which was more true than logical. Most of these
men had commenced life with a stern declaration of
war against the forest; and, although the men usually
won at last, the battle was a long and hard one.
Small wonder that they came to look upon a forest
tree as a natural enemy. The camp-fire question
came to a crisis, however, with two or three of these
old settlers. And, as the story well illustrates my
point, I will venture to tell it.

It was in the "dark days before Christmas" that a
party of four started from W., bound for a camp on
Second Fork, in the deepest part of the wilderness
that lies between Wellsboro and the Block.House.
The party consisted of Sile J., Old Al., Eli J. and
the writer. The two first were gray-haired men,
the others past thirty; all the same, they called us
"the boys." The weather was not inviting, and there
was small danger of our camp being invaded by
summer outers or tenderfeet. It cost twelve miles of
hard travel to reach that camp; and, though we
started at daylight, it was past noon when we arrived.
The first seven miles could be made on wheels, the
balance by hard tramping. The road was execrable;
no one cared to ride; but it was necessary to have
our loads carried as far as possible. The clearings
looked dreary enough, and the woods forbidding to
a degree, but our old camp was the picture of desolation. There was six inches of damp snow on the
leafless brush roof, the blackened brands of our last
fire were sticking their charred ends out of the snow,

the hemlocks were bending sadly under their loads of wet snow, and the entire surroundings had a cold, cheerless, slushy look, very little like the ideal hunter's camp. We placed our knapsacks in the shanty, Eli got out his nail hatchet, I drew my little pocket-axe, and we proceeded to start a fire, while the two older men went up stream a few rods to unearth a full-grown axe and a bottle of old rye, which they had *cached* under a log three months before. They never fooled with pocket-axes. They were gone so long that we sauntered up the bank, thinking it might be the rye that detained them. We found them with their coats off, working like beavers, each with a stout, sharpened stick. There had been an October freshet, and a flood-jam at the bend had sent the mad stream over its banks, washing the log out of position and piling a gravel bar two feet deep over the spot where the axe and flask should have been. About the only thing left to do was to cut a couple of stout sticks, organize a mining company, limited, and go in; which they did. Sile was drifting into the side of the sandbar savagely, trying to strike the axe-helve, and old Al. was sinking numberless miniature shafts from the surface in a vain attempt to strike whisky. The company failed in about half an hour. Sile resumed his coat, and sat down on a log—which was one of his best holds, by the way. He looked at Al.; Al. looked at him; then both looked at us, and Sile remarked that, if one of the boys wanted to go out to the clearings and "borry" an axe; and come back in the morning, he thought the others could pick up wood enough to tough it out one night. Of course nobody could stay in an open winter camp without an axe.

CAMP-FIRE AS IT SHOULD BE MADE.

It was my time to come to the front. I said: "You two just go at the camp; clean the snow off and slick up the inside. Put my shelter-cloth with Eli's, and cover the roof with them; and if you don't have just

as good a fire to-night as you ever had, you can tie
me to a beech and leave me there. Come on, Eli."
And Eli did come on. And this is how we did it:
We first felled a thrifty butternut tree ten inches in
diameter, cut off three lengths of five feet each, and
carried them to camp. These were the back logs.
Two stout stakes were driven at the back of the fire,
and the logs, on top of each other, were laid firmly
against the stakes. The latter were slanted a little
back, and the largest log placed at bottom, the smallest on top, to prevent tipping forward. A couple of
short, thick sticks were laid with the ends against the
bottom log by way of fire dogs; a fore stick, five feet
long and five inches in diameter; a well built pyramid
of bark, knots and small logs completed the camp-
fire, which sent a pleasant glow of warmth and heat
to the furthest corner of the shanty. For "night-
wood," we cut a dozen birch and ash poles from four
to six inches across, trimmed them to the tips, and
dragged them to camp. Then we denuded a dry
hemlock of its bark by aid of ten-foot poles, flattened
at one end, and packed the bark to camp. We had
a bright, cheery fire from the early evening until
morning, and four tired hunters never slept more
soundly.

We staid in that camp a week; and, though the
weather was rough and cold, the little pocket-axes
kept us well in firewood. We selected butternut for
back logs, because, when green, it burns very slowly
and lasts a long time. And we dragged our smaller
wood to camp in lengths of twenty to thirty feet, be-

cause it was easier to lay them on the fire and "nigger" them in two than to cut them shorter with light hatchets. With a heavy axe, we should have cut them to lengths of five or six feet.

Our luck, I may mention, was good—as good as we desired. Not that four smallish deer are anything to brag of for a week's hunt by four men and two dogs. I have known a pot-hunter to kill nine in a single day. But we had enough.

As it was, we were obliged to "double trip it" in order to get our deer and duffle down to "Babb's." And we gave away more than half our venison. For the rest, the illustrations show the camp-fire—all but the fire—as it should be made.

CHAPTER V.

FISHING, WITH AND WITHOUT FLIES.—SOME TACKLE
AND LURES. — DISCURSIVE REMARKS ON THE
GENTLE ART.—THE HEADLIGHT.—FROGGING.

THERE is probably no subject connected with
out-door sport so thoroughly and exhaustively
written up as fly-fishing, and all that pertains thereto.
Fly-fishing for speckled trout always, and deservedly,
takes the lead. Bass fishing usually comes next,
though some writers accord second place to the lake
trout, salmon trout or land-locked salmon. The
mascalonge, as a game fish, is scarcely behind the
small-mouthed bass, and is certainly more gamy than
the lake trout. The large-mouthed bass and pickerel are usually ranked about with the yellow perch.
I don't know why; they are certainly gamy enough.
Perhaps it is because they do not leap out of water
when hooked. Both are good on the table.

A dozen able and interesting authors have written
books wherein trout, flies and fly-fishing are treated
in a manner that leaves an old backwoodsman little
to say. Rods, reels, casting lines, flies and fish are described and descanted on in a way, and in a language,
the reading whereof reduces me to temporary insanity.

And yet I seem to recollect some bygone incidents concerning fish and fishing. I have a well defined notion that I once stood on Flat Rock, in Big Pine Creek, and caught over 350 fine trout in a short day's fishing. Also, that many times I left home on a bright May or June morning, walked eight miles, caught a twelve-pound creel of trout, and walked home before bedtime.

I remember that once, in Michigan, on the advice of local fishermen, I dragged a spoon around High Bank Lake for two days, with little result save half a dozen blisters on my hands; and that on the next morning, taking a long tamarack pole and my own way of fishing, I caught, before 10 A. M., fifty pounds of bass and pickerel, weighing from two to ten pounds each. Gibson, whose spoon, line and skiff I had been using and who was the fishing oracle of that region, could hardly believe his eyes. I kept that country inn, and the neighborhood as well, supplied with fish for the next two weeks.

It is truth to say that I have never struck salt or fresh waters, where edible fish were at all plenty, without being able to take, in some way, all that I needed. Notably and preferably with the fly if that might be. If not, then with worms, grubs, minnows, grasshoppers, crickets, or any sort of doodle bug their highnesses might affect. When a plump, two-pound trout refuses to eat a tinseled, feathered fraud, I am not the man to refuse him something more edible.

That I may not be misunderstood, let me say that

I recognize the speckled brook trout as the very emperor of all game fish, and angling for him with the fly as the neatest, most fascinating sport attainable by the angler. But there are thousands of outers who, from choice or necessity, take their summer vacations where *Salmo fontinalis* is not to be had. They would prefer him, either on the leader or the table; but he is not there; "And a man has got a stomach, and we live by what we eat."

Wherefore, they go a-fishing for other fish. So that they are successful and sufficiently fed, the difference is not so material. I have enjoyed myself hugely catching catties on a dark night from a skiff, with a hand-line.

I can add nothing in a scientific way to the literature of fly-fishing; but I can give a few hints that may be conducive to practical success, as well with trout as with less noble fish. In fly-fishing, one serviceable ten-ounce rod is enough; and a plain click reel, of small size, is just as satisfactory as a more costly affair. Twenty yards of tapered, water-proof line, with a six-foot leader, and a cast of two flies, complete the rig, and will be found sufficient. In common with most fly-fishers, I have mostly thrown a cast of three flies, but have found two just as effective, and handier.

We all carry too many flies. Some of my friends have more than sixty dozen, and will never use a tenth of them. In the summer of '83, finding I had more than seemed needful, I left all but four dozen behind me. I wet only fifteen of them in a seven

weeks' outing. And they filled the bill. I have no
time or space for a dissertation on the hundreds of
different flies made and sold at the present day.
Abler pens have done that. I will, however, name a
few that I have found good in widely different localities, *i. e.*, the Northern Wilderness of New York and
the upper waters of Northern Pennsylvania. For
the Northern Wilderness: Scarlet ibis, split ibis, Ro-
meyn, white-winged coachman, royal coachman, red
hackle, red-bodied ashy and gray-bodied ashy. The
ashies were good for black bass also. For Northern
Pennsylvania: Queen of the waters, professor, red
fox, coachman, black may, white-winged coachman,
wasp, brown hackle, Seth Green. Ibis flies are worth-
less here. Using the dark flies in bright water and
clear weather, and the brighter colors for evening,
the list was long enough.

At the commencement of the open season, and
until the young maple leaves are half grown, bait
will be found far more successful than the fly. At
this time the trout are pretty evenly distributed along
lake shores and streams, choosing to lie quietly in
rather deep pools, and avoiding swift water. A few
may rise to the fly in a logy, indifferent way; but the
best way to take them is bait-fishing with well-cleansed
angle worms or white grubs, the latter being the best
bait I have ever tried. They take the bait sluggishly
at this season, but, on feeling the hook, wake up to
their normal activity and fight gamely to the last.
When young, new-born insects begin to drop freely
on the water, about the 20th of May, trout leave the

pools and take to the riffles. And from this time until the latter part of June the fly-fisherman is in his glory. It may be true that the skillful bait-fisherman will rather beat his creel. He cares not for that. He can take enough; and he had rather take ten trout with the fly than a score with bait. As for the man who goes a-fishing simply to catch fish, the fly-fisher does not recognize him as an angler at all.

When the sun is hot and the weather grows warm, trout leave the ripples and take to cold springs and spring-holes; the largest fish, of course, monopolizing the deepest and coolest places, while the smaller ones hover around, or content themselves with shallower water. As the weather gets hotter, the fly-fishing falls off badly. A few trout of four to eight ounces in weight may still be raised, but the larger ones are lying on the bottom, and are not to be fooled with feathers. They will take a tempting bait when held before their noses—sometimes; at other times, not. As to raising them with a fly—as well attempt to raise a sick Indian with the temperance pledge. And yet, they may be taken in bright daylight by a ruse that I learned long ago, of a youngster less than half my age, a little, freckled, thin-visaged young man, whose health was evidently affected by a daily struggle with a pair of tow-colored side whiskers and a light moustache. There was hardly enough of the whole affair to make a door-mat for a bee hive. But he seemed so proud of the plant, that I forbore to rig him. He was better than he looked—as often happens. The landlord said, "He brings in large trout

every day, when our best fly-fishermen fail." One
night, around an out-door fire, we got acquainted,
and I found him a witty, pleasant companion. Before
turning in I ventured to ask him how he succeeded in
taking large trout, while the experts only caught
small ones, or failed altogether.

"Go with me to-morrow morning to a spring-hole
three miles up the river, and I'll show you," he said.

Of course, we went. He, rowing a light skiff, and
paddling a still lighter canoe. The spring-hole
was in a narrow bay that set back from the river, and
at the mouth of a cold, clear brook; it was ten to
twelve feet deep, and at the lower end a large balsam
had fallen in with the top in just the right place for
getting away with large fish, or tangling lines and
leaders. We moored some twenty feet above the
spring-hole, and commenced fishing. I with my
favorite cast of flies, my friend with the tail of a minnow. He caught a 1½-pound trout almost at the
outset, but I got no rise; did not expect it. Then I
went above, where the water was shallower, and
raised a couple of half-pounders, but could get no
more. I thought we had better go to the hotel with
what we had, but my friend said "wait;" he went
ashore and picked up a long pole with a bushy tip;
it had evidently been used before. Dropping down
to the spring-hole, he thrust the tip to the bottom and
slashed it around in a way to scare and scatter every
trout within a hundred feet.

"And what does all that mean?" I asked.

"Well," he said, "every trout will be back in less

than an hour; and when they first come back, they take the bait greedily. Better take off your leader and try bait."

Which I did. Dropping our hooks to the bottom, we waited some twenty minutes, when we had a bite, and, having strong tackle, soon took in a trout that turned the scale at 2¼ pounds. Then my turn came and I saved one weighing 1½ pounds. He caught another of 1¼ pounds, and I took one of 1 pound. Then they ceased biting altogether.

"And now," said my friend, "if you will work your canoe carefully around to that old balsam top and get the light where you can see the bottom, you may see some large trout."

I did as directed, and, making a telescope of my hand, looked intently for the bottom of the spring-hole. At first I could see nothing but water; then I made out some dead sticks, and finally began to dimly trace the outlines of large fish. There they were, more than forty of them, lying quietly on the bottom like suckers, but genuine brook trout, every one of them.

"This," said he, "makes the fifth time I have brushed them out of here, and I have never missed taking from two to five large trout. I have two other places where I always get one or two, but this is the best."

At the hotel we found two fly-fishers who had been out all the morning. They each had three or four small trout.

During the next week we worked the spring-holes

daily in the same way, and always with success. I have also had good success by building a bright fire on the bank, and fishing a spring-hole by the light—a mode of fishing especially successful with catties and perch.

A bright, bullseye headlight, strapped on a stiff hat, so that the light can be thrown where it is wanted, is an excellent device for night fishing. And during the heated term, when fish are slow and sluggish, I have found the following plan work well: Bake a hard, well salted, water "johnny-cake," break it into pieces the size of a hen's egg, and drop the pieces into a spring-hole. This calls a host of minnows, and the larger fish follow the minnows. It will prove more successful on perch, catties, chubs, etc., than on trout, however. By this plan, I have kept a camp of five men well supplied with fish when their best flies failed—as they mostly do in very hot weather.

Fishing for mascalonge, pickerel, and bass, is quite another thing, though by many valued as a sport scarcely inferior to fly-fishing for trout. I claim no especial skill with the fly-rod. It is a good day when I get my tail fly more than fifteen yards beyond the reel, with any degree of accuracy.

My success lies mainly with the tribes of *Esox* and *Micropterus*. Among these, I have seldom or never failed during the last thirty-six years, when the water was free of ice; and I have had just as good luck when big-mouthed bass and pickerel were in the "off season," as at any time. For in many waters there comes a time—in late August and September—when neither bass nor pickerel will notice the spoon, be it handled never so wisely. Even the mascalonge looks on the flashing cheat with indifference; though a very hungry specimen may occasionally immolate himself. It was at such a season that I fished High Bank Lake—as before mentioned—catching from forty to fifty pounds of fine fish every morning for nearly two weeks, after the best local fishermen had assured me that not a decent sized fish could be taken at that season. Perhaps a brief description of the modes and means that have proved invariably successful for many years may afford a few useful hints, even to old anglers.

To begin with, I utterly discard all modern "gangs" and "trains," carrying from seven to thirteen hooks each. They are all too small, and all too many; better calculated to scratch and tear, than to catch and hold. Three hooks are enough at the end of any line, and better than more. These should be fined or honed to a perfect point, and the abrupt part of the barb filed down one-half. All hooks, as usually made, have twice as much barb as they should have; and the sharp bend of the barb prevents the entering of the hook in hard bony structures, wherefore the fish only stays hooked so long as there is a taut pull on the line. A little loosening of the line and one shake of the head sets him free. But no fish can shake out a hook well sunken in mouth or gills, though two-thirds of the barb be filed away.

For mascalonge or pickerel I invariably use wire

snells made as follows: Lay off four or more strands
of fine brass wire 13 inches long; turn one end of the

FROG-BAIT.   THREE-HOOK GANGS.

wires smoothly over a No. 1 iron wire, and work the
ends in between the strands below.   Now, with a pair
of pincers hold the ends, and, using No. 1 as a

handle, twist the ends and body of the snell firmly together; this gives the loop; next, twist the snell evenly
and strongly from end to end. Wax the end of the
snell thoroughly for two or three inches, and wax the
tapers of two strong Sproat or O'Shaughnessy hooks,
and wind the lower hook on with strong, waxed silk,
to the end of the taper; then lay the second hook at
right angles with the first, and one inch above it;
wind this as the other, and then fasten a third and
smaller hook above that for a lip hook. This gives
a snell about one foot in length, with the two lower
hooks standing at right angles, one above the other,
and a third and smaller hook in line with the second.

The bait is the element of success; it is made as
follows: Slice off a clean, white pork rind, four or
five inches long, by an inch and a half wide; lay it on
a board, and, with a sharp knife cut it as nearly to
the shape of a frog as your ingenuity permits. Prick
a slight gash in the head to admit the lip hook, which
should be an inch and a half above the second one,
and see that the fork of the bait rests securely in the
barb of the middle hook.

Use a stout bait-rod and strong line. Fish from a
boat, with a second man to handle the oars, if convenient. Let the oarsman lay the boat ten feet inside
the edge of the lily-pads, and make your cast, say,
with thirty feet of line; land the bait neatly to the right,
at the edge of the lily-pads, let it sink a few inches,
and then with the tip well lowered; bring the bait
around on a slight curve by a quick succession of
draws, with a momentary pause between each; the

object being to imitate as nearly as possible a swimming frog. If this be neatly done, and if the bait be made as it should be, at every short halt the legs will spread naturally, and the imitation is perfect enough to deceive the most experienced bass or pickerel. When half a dozen casts to right and left have been made without success, it is best to move on, still keeping inside and casting outside the lily-pads.

A pickerel of three pounds or more will take in all three hooks at the first snap; and, as he closes his mouth tightly and starts for the bottom, strike quickly, but not too hard, and let the boatman put you out into deep water at once, where you are safe from the strong roots of the yellow lily.

It is logically certain your fish is well hooked. You cannot pull two strong, sharp hooks through that tightly closed mouth without fastening at least one of them where it will do most good. Oftener both will catch, and it frequently happens that one hook will catch each lip, holding the mouth nearly closed, and shortening the struggles of a large fish very materially. On taking off a fish, and before casting again, see that the two lower hooks stand at right angles. If they have got turned in the struggle you can turn them to any angle you like; the twisted wire is stiff enough to hold them in place. Every angler knows the bold, determined manner in which the mascalonge strikes his prey. He will take in bait and hooks at the first dash, and if the rod be held stiffly, usually hooks himself. Barring large trout, he is the king of game fish. The big-mouthed bass is less savage in his attacks, but is a free biter. He is apt to come up behind and seize the bait about two-thirds of its length, turn, and bore down for the bottom. He will mostly take in the lower hooks, however, and is certain to get fastened. His large mouth is excellent for retaining the hook.

As for the small-mouthed (*Micropterus dolomieu,* if you want to be scientific), I have found him more capricious than any game fish on the list. One day he will take only dobsons, or crawfish; the next, he may prefer minnows, and again, he will rise to the fly or a feathered spoon.

On the whole, I have found the pork frog the most successful lure in his case; but the hooks and bait must be arranged differently. Three strands of fine wire will make a snell strong enough, and the hooks should be strong, sharp and rather small, the lower hooks placed only half an inch apart, and a small lip hook two and a quarter inches above the middle one. As the fork of the bait will not reach the bend of the middle hook, it must be fastened to the snell by a few stitches taken with stout thread, and the lower end of the bait should not reach more than a quarter of an inch beyond the bottom of the hook, because the small-mouth has a villainous trick of giving his prey a stern chase, nipping constantly and viciously at the tail, and the above arrangement will be apt to hook him at the first snap. Owing to this trait, some artificial minnows with one or two hooks at the caudal end, are very killing—when he will take them.

Lake, or salmon trout, may be trolled for success-fully with the above lure; but I do not much affect fishing for them. Excellent sport may be had with them, however, early in the season, when they are working near the shore, but they soon retire to water from fifty to seventy feet deep, and can only be caught by deep trolling or buoy-fishing. I have no fancy for sitting in a slow-moving boat for hours, dragging three or four hundred feet of line in deep water, a four-pound sinker tied by six feet of lighter line some twenty feet above the hooks. The sinker is supposed to go bumping along the bottom, while the bait follows three or four feet above it. The drag of the long line and the constant jogging of the sinker on rocks and snags, make it difficult to tell when one has a strike—and it is always too long between bites.

Sitting for hours at a baited buoy with a hand-line, and without taking a fish, is still worse, as more than once I have been compelled to acknowledge in very weariness of soul. There are enthusiastic anglers, however, whose specialty is trolling for lake trout. A gentleman by the name of Thatcher, who has a fine residence on Raquette Lake—which he calls a camp —makes this his leading sport, and keeps a log of his fishing, putting nothing on record of less than ten pounds weight. His largest fish was booked at twenty-eight pounds, and he added that a well-conditioned salmon trout was superior to a brook trout on the table; in which I quite agree with him. But he seemed quite disgusted when I ventured to suggest that a well-conditioned cattie or bullhead, caught in the same waters—was better than either.

"Do you call the cattie a game fish?" he asked.

Yes; I call any fish a game fish that is taken for sport with hook and line. I can no more explain the common prejudice against the catfish and eel than I can tell why an experienced angler should drag a gang of thirteen hooks through the water—ten of them being worse than superfluous. "Frank Forester" gives five hooks as the number for a trolling gang. We mostly use hooks too small, and do not look after points and barbs closely enough. A pair of No. 1 O'Shaughnessy, or 1½ Sproat, or five tapered black-fish hooks, will make a killing rig for small-mouthed bass, using No. 4 Sproat for lip hook. Larger hooks are better for the big-mouthed, a four-pound specimen of which will easily take in one's fist. A pair of 5-0 O'Shaughnessys, or Sproats will be found none too large; and as for the mascalonge and pickerel, if I must err, let it be on the side of large hooks and strong lines.

It is idle to talk of playing the fish in water where the giving of a few yards insures a hopeless tangle among roots, tree-tops, etc. I was once fishing in Western waters where the pickerel ran very large, and I used a pair of the largest salmon hooks with tackle strong enough to hold a fish of fifteen pounds, without any playing; notwithstanding which, I had five trains of three hooks each taken off in as many days by monster pickerel. An expert mascalonge fisher-man—Davis by name—happened to take board at the farm house where I was staying, and he had a notion that he could "beat some of them big fellows;" and he did it; did it with three large cod hooks, a bit of fine, strong chain, twelve yards of cod-line, an eighteen-foot tamarack pole, and a twelve-inch sucker for bait. I thought it the most outlandish rig I had ever seen, but went with him in the early gray of the morning to see it tried, just where I had lost my hooks and fish.

Raising the heavy bait in the air, he would give it a whirl to gather headway, and launch it forty feet away with a splash that might have been heard thirty rods. It looked more likely to scare than catch, but was a success. At the third or fourth cast we plainly saw a huge pickerel rise, shut his immense mouth over bait, hooks, and a few inches of chain, turn lazily, and head for the bottom, where Mr. D. let him rest a minute, and then struck steadily but strongly. The subsequent struggle depended largely on main strength, though there was a good deal of skill and cool judgment shown in the handling and landing of the fish. A pickerel of forty pounds or more is not to be snatched out of the water on his first mad rush; something must be yielded—and with no reel there is little chance of giving line. It struck me my friend managed his fish remarkably well, towing him back and forth with a strong pull, never giving him a rest and finally sliding him out on a low muddy bank, as though he were a smooth log. We took him up to the house and tested the size of his mouth by putting a quart cup in it, which went in easily. Then we weighed him, and he turned the scales at forty-four pounds. It was some consolation to find three of my hooks sticking in his mouth. Lastly, we had a large section of him stuffed and baked. It was good; but a ten-pound fish would have been better. The moral of all this—if it has any moral—is, use hooks according to the size of fish you expect to catch.

And, when you are in a permanent camp, and fishing is very poor, try frogging. It is not sport of a high order, though it may be called angling—and it can be made amusing, with hook and line. I have seen educated ladies in the wilderness, fishing for frogs with an eagerness and enthusiasm not surpassed by the most devoted angler with his favorite cast of flies. There are several modes of taking the festive batrachian. He is speared with a frog-spear; caught under the chin with snatch-hooks; taken with hook and line, or picked up from a canoe with the aid of a headlight, or jack-lamp. The two latter modes are best.

To take him with hook and line; a light rod, six to eight feet of line, a snell of single gut with a 1-o Sproat or O'Shaughnessy hook, and a bit of bright scarlet flannel for bait; this is the rig. To use it, paddle up behind him silently, and drop the rag just in front of his nose. He is pretty certain to take it on the instant. Knock him on the head before cutting off his legs. It is unpleasant to see him squirm, and hear him cry like a child while you are sawing at his thigh joints.

By far the most effective manner of frogging is by

the headlight on dark nights. To do this most successfully, one man in a light canoe, a good headlight and a light, one-handed paddle, are the requirements. The frog is easily located, either by his croaking, or by his peculiar shape. Paddle up to him silently and throw the light in his eyes; you may then pick him up as you would a potato. I have known a North Woods guide to pick up a five-quart pail of frogs in an hour, on a dark evening. On the table, frogs' legs are usually conceded first place for delicacy and flavor. For an appetizing breakfast in camp, they have no equal, in my judgment. The high price they bring at the best hotels, and their growing scarcity, attest the value placed on them by men who know how and what to eat. And, not many years ago, an old pork-gobbling backwoodsman threw his frying-pan into the river because I had cooked frogs' legs in it. While another, equally intelligent, refused to use my frying-pan, because I had cooked eels in it; remarking sententiously, "Eels is snakes, an' I know it."

It may be well, just here and now, to say a word on the importance of the headlight. I know of no more pleasant and satisfactory adjunct of a camp than a good light that can be adjusted to the head, used as a jack in floating, carried in the hand, or fastened up inside the shanty. Once fairly tried, it will never be ignored or forgotten. Not that it will show a deer's head seventeen rods distant with sufficient clearness for a shot—or your sights with distinctness enough to make it. (See Murray's Adirondacks, page 174.)

A headlight that will show a deer plainly at six rods, while lighting the sights of a rifle with clearness, is an exceptionally good light. More deer are killed in floating under than over four rods. There are various styles of headlights, jack-lamps, etc., in use; but the best I know anything about are advertised by Ferguson, 65 Fulton street, New York. They are bright, easily adjusted, and will show rifle sights, or a deer, up to 100 feet—which is enough. They are also convenient in camp, and better than a lantern on a dim forest path.

Before leaving the subject of bait-fishing, I have a point or two I wish to make. I have attempted to explain the frog-bait, and the manner of using it, and I shall probably never have occasion to change my belief that it is, on the whole, the most killing lure for the entire tribes of bass and pickerel. There is, however, another, which, if properly handled, is almost as good. It is as follows:

Take a bass, pickerel, or yellow perch, of one pound or less; scrape the scales clean on the under side from the caudal fin to a point just forward of the vent. Next, with a sharp knife, cut up toward the backbone, commencing just behind the vent with a slant toward the tail. Run the knife smoothly along just under the backbone, and out through the caudal fin, taking about one-third of the latter, and making a clean, white bait, with the anal and a part of the caudal by way of fins. It looks very like a white minnow in the water; but is better, in that it is more showy, and infinitely tougher. A minnow soon drags to pieces. To use it, two strong hooks are tied on a wire snell at right angles, the upper one an inch above the lower, and the upper hook is passed through the bait, leaving it to draw without turning or spinning. The casting and handling is the same as with the frog-bait, and it is very killing for bass, pickerel, and mascalonge. It is a good lure for salmon trout also; but, for him it was found better to fasten the bait with the lower hook in a way to give it a spinning motion; and this necessitates the use of a swivel, which I do not like; because, "a rope is as strong as its weakest part;" and I have more than once found that weakest part the swivel. If, however, a swivel has been tested by a dead lift of twenty to twenty-five pounds, it will do to trust.

I have spoken only of brass or copper wire for snells, and for pickerel or mascalonge of large size nothing else is to be depended on. But for trout and bass, strong gut or gimp is safe enough. The possibilities as to size of the mascalonge and Northern pickerel no man knows. Frank Forester thinks it probable that the former attains to the weight of sixty to eighty pounds, while he only accords the pickerel a weight of seventeen to eighteen pounds. I have seen several pickerel of over forty pounds, and one that turned the scale at fifty-three. And I saw a mascalonge on Georgian Bay that was longer than the Canuck guide who was toting the fish over his shoulder by a stick thrust in the mouth and gills. The snout reached to the top of the guide's head, while the caudal fin dragged on the ground. There was no chance for weighing the fish, but I hefted him several times, carefully, and am certain he weighed more than a bushel of wheat. Just what tackle would be proper for such a powerful fellow I am not prepared to say, having lost the largest specimens I ever hooked. My best mascalonge weighed less than twenty pounds. My largest pickerel still less.

I will close this discursive chapter by offering a bit of advice. Do not go into the woods on a fishing tour without a stock of well cleansed angle-worms. Keep them in a tin can partly filled with damp moss, and in a cool, moist place. There is no one variety of bait that the angler finds so constantly useful as the worm. Izaak Walton by no means despised worme or bait-fishing.

CHAPTER VI.

CAMP COOKERY.—HOW IT IS USUALLY DONE, WITH A
FEW SIMPLE HINTS ON PLAIN COOKING.—COOK-
ING FIRE AND OUT-DOOR RANGE.

THE way in which an average party of summer
outers will contrive to manage—or mis-man-
age—the camp and camp-fire so as to get the greatest
amount of smoke and discomfort at the least outlay
of time and force, is something past all understanding,
and somewhat aggravating to an old woodsman who
knows some better. But it is just as good fun as the
cynical O. W. can ask, to see a party of three or four
enthusiastic youngsters organize the camp on the first
day in, and proceed to cook the first meal. Of course,
every man is boss, and every one is bound to build
the fire, which every one proceeds to do. There are
no back logs, no fore sticks, and no arrangements for
level, solid bases on which to place frying-pans, coffee
pots, etc. But, there is a sufficiency of knots, dry
sticks, bark and chunks, with some kindling at the
bottom, and a heavy volume of smoke working its
way through the awkward-looking pile. Presently
thin tongues of blue flame begin to shoot up through
the interstices, and four bran new coffee pots are

wriggled into level positions at as many different points on the bonfire. Four hungry youngsters commence slicing ham and pork, four frying-pans are brought out from as many hinged and lidded soap boxes—when one man yells out hurriedly, "Look out, Joe, there's your coffee pot handle coming off." And he drops his frying-pan to save his coffee pot, which he does, minus the spout and handle. Then it is seen that the flames have increased rapidly, and all the pots are in danger. A short, sharp skirmish rescues them, at the expense of some burned fingers, and culinary operations are the order of the hour.

Coffee and tea are brewed with the loss of a handle or two, and the frying-pans succeed in scorching the pork and ham to an unwholesome black mess. The potato kettle does better. It is not easy to spoil potatoes by cooking them in plenty of boiling water; and, as there is plenty of bread with fresh butter, not to mention canned goods, the hungry party feed sufficiently, but not satisfactorily. Everything seems pervaded with smoke. The meat is scorched bitter, and the tea is of the sort described by Charles Dudley Warner, in his humorous description of "Camping Out": "The sort of tea that takes hold, lifts the hair, and disposes the drinker to hilariouness. There is no deception about it, it tastes of tannin, and spruce, and creosote." Of the cooking he says: "Everything has been cooked in a tin pail and a skillet—potatoes, tea, pork, mutton, slapjacks. You wonder how everything could have been prepared in so few utensils. When you eat, the wonder ceases, everything might

have been cooked in one pail. It is a noble meal.
* * * The slapjacks are a solid job of work, made
to last, and not go to pieces in a person's stomach like
a trivial bun."

I have before me a copy of *Forest and Stream*, in
which the canoe editor, under the heading of "The
Galley Fire," has some remarks well worth quoting.
He says: "The question of camp cookery is one of
the greatest importance to all readers of *Forest and
Stream*, but most of all to the canoeists and * * *
the Corinthian sailor. * * * From ignorance of
what to carry, the canoeist falls back on canned goods,
never healthy as a steady diet, Brunswick soups and
eggs. * * * The misery of that first camp-fire,
who has forgotten it? Tired, hungry, perhaps cold
and wet, the smoke everywhere, the coffee pot melted
down, the can of soup upset in the fire, the fiendish
conduct of frying-pan and kettle, the final surrender
of the exhausted victim, sliding off to sleep with a
piece of hardtack in one hand and a slice of canned
beef in the other, only to dream of mother's hot
biscuits, juicy steaks, etc., etc." It is very well put,
and so true to the life. And again: "Frying, baking, making coffee, stews, plain biscuit, the neat and
speedy preparation of a healthy 'square meal' can be
easily learned." Aye, and should be learned by
every man who goes to the woods with or without a
canoe.

But, I was describing a first day's camping out, the
party being four young men and one old woodsman,
the latter going along in a double character of invited

guest and amateur guide. When the boys are through
with their late dinner, they hustle the greasy frying-
pans and demoralized tinware into a corner of the
shanty, and get out their rods for an evening's fishing.
They do it hurriedly, almost feverishly, as youngsters
are apt to do at the start. The O. W. has taken no
part in the dinner, and has said nothing save in re-
sponse to direct questions, nor has he done anything
to keep up his reputation as a woodsman, except to
see that the shelter roof is properly put up and fastened. Having seen to this, he reverts to his favorite
pastime, sitting on a log and smoking navy plug.
Long experience has taught him that it is best to let
the boys effervesce a little. They will slop over a
trifle at first, but twenty-four hours will settle them.
When they are fairly out of hearing, he takes the old
knapsack from the clipped limb where it has been
hung, cuts a slice of ham, butters a slice of bread,
spreads the live coals and embers, makes a pot of
strong green tea, broils the ham on a three-pronged
birch fork, and has a clean, well-cooked, plain dinner.
Then he takes the sharp three-pound camp axe, and
fells a dozen small birch and ash trees, cutting them
into proper lengths and leaving them for the boys to
tote into camp. Next, a bushy, heavy-topped hemlock is felled, and the O. W. proceeds leisurely to pick
a heap of fine hemlock browse. A few handfuls suf-
fice to stuff the muslin pillow bag, and the rest is carefully spread on the port side of the shanty for a bed.
The pillow is placed at the head, and the old Mack-
inac blanket-bag is spread neatly over all, as a token

of ownership and possession. If the youngsters want beds of fine, elastic browse, let 'em make their own beds.

No camp-fire should be without poker and tongs. The poker is a beech stick four feet long by two inches thick, flattened at one end, with a notch cut in it for lifting kettles, etc. To make the tongs, take a tough beech or hickory stick, one inch thick by two feet in length, shave it down nearly one-half for a foot in the center, thrust this part into hot embers until it bends freely, bring the ends together and whittle them smoothly to a fit on the inside, cross-checking them also to give them a grip; finish off by chamfering the ends neatly from the outside. They will be found exceedingly handy in rescuing a bit of tinware, a slice of steak or ham, or any small article that happens to get dropped in a hot fire.

And don't neglect the camp broom. It is made by laying bushy hemlock twigs around a light handle, winding them firmly with strong twine or moose wood bark, and chopping off the ends of the twigs evenly. It can be made in ten minutes. Use it to brush any leaves, sticks, and any litter from about the camp or fire. Neatness is quite as pleasant and wholesome around the forest camp as in the home kitchen. These little details may seem trivial to the reader. But remember, if there is a spot on earth where trifles make up the sum of human enjoyment, it is to be found in a woodland camp. All of which the O. W. fully appreciates, as he finishes the above little jobs: after which he proceeds to spread the fire to a broad level bed of glowing embers, nearly covering the same with small pieces of hemlock bark, that the boys may have a decent cooking fire on their return.

About sundown they come straggling in, not jubilant and hilarious, footsore rather and a little cross. The effervescence is subsiding, and the noise is pretty well knocked out of them. They have caught and dressed some three score of small brook trout, which they deposit beside the shanty, and proceed at once to move on the fire, with evident intent of raising a conflagration, but are checked by the O. W., who calls their attention to the fact that for all culinary purposes, the fire is about as near the right thing as they are likely to get it. Better defer the bonfire until after supper. Listening to the voice of enlightened woodcraft, they manage to fry trout and make tea without scorch or creosote, and the supper is a decided improvement on the dinner. But the dishes are piled away as before, without washing.

Then follows an hour of busy work, bringing wood to camp and picking browse. The wood is sufficient; but the brows is picked, or cut, all too coarse, and there is only enough of it to make the camp look green and pleasant—not enough to rest weary shoulders and backs. But, they are sound on the bonfire. They pile on the wood in the usual way, criss-cross and hap-hazard. It makes a grand fire, that lights up the forest for fifty yards around, and the tired youngsters turn in. Having the advantage of driving a team to the camping ground, they are well supplied with blankets and robes. They ought to sleep soundly, but they don't. The usual draw-backs of a first night in camp are soon manifested in uneasy twistings and turnings, grumbling at stubs, knots, and sticks, that utterly ignore conformity with the angles of the human frame. But at last, tired nature asserts her supremacy, and they sleep. Sleep soundly, for a couple of hours; when the bonfire, having reached the point of disintegration, suddenly collapses with a sputtering and crackling that brings them to their head's antipodes, and four dazed, sleepy faces, look out with a bewildered air, to see what has caused the rumpus. All take a hand in putting the brands together and re-arranging the fire, which burns better than at first; some sleepy talk, one or two feeble attempts at a smoke, and they turn in again. But, there is not an hour during the remainder of the night in which some one is not pot-tering about the fire.

The O. W., who has abided by his blanket-bag all night—quietly taking in the fun—rouses out the party at 4 A. M. For two of them are to fish Asaph Run with bait, and the other two are to try the riffles of Marsh Creek with the fly. As the wood is all burned to cinders and glowing coals, there is no chance for a smoky fire; and, substituting coffee for tea, the breakfast is a repetition of the supper.

By sunrise the boys are off, and the O. W. has the camp to himself. He takes it leisurely, gets up a neat breakfast of trout, bread, butter, and coffee, cleans and puts away his dishes, has a smoke, and picks up the camp axe. Selecting a bushy hemlock fifteen inches across, he lets it down in as many minutes, trims it to the very tip, piles the limbs in a heap, and cuts three lengths of six feet each from the butt. This insures browse and back logs for some time ahead. Two strong stakes are cut and sharpened. Four small logs, two of eight, and two of nine feet in length, are prepared, plenty of night wood is made ready, a supply of bright, dry hemlock bark is carried to camp, and the O. W. rests from his labors, resuming his favorite pastime of sitting on a log and smoking navy plug. Finally it occurs to him that he is there partly as guide and mentor to the younger men, and that they need a lesson on cleanliness. He brings out the frying-pans and finds a filthy-looking mess of grease in each one, wherein ants, flies, and other insects have contrived to get mixed. Does he heat some water, and clean and scour the pans? Not if he knows himself. If he did it once he might keep on doing it. He is cautious about establishing precedents, and he has a taste for entomology. He places the pans in the sun where the grease will soften and goes skirmishing for ants and doodle bugs. They are not far to seek, and he soon has a score of large black ants, with a few bugs and spiders, pretty equally distributed among the frying-pans. To give the thing a plausible look a few flies are added, and the two largest pans are finished off, one with a large ear wig, the other with a thousand-legged worm. The pans are replaced in the shanty, the embers are leveled and nearly covered with bits of dry hemlock bark, and the O. W. resumes his pipe and log,

"With such a face of Christian satisfaction,
As good men wear, who have done a virtuous action."

Before noon the boys are all in, and as the catch is twice as numerous and twice as large as on the previous evening, and as the weather is all that could be asked of the longest days in June, they are in excellent spirits. The boxes are brought out, pork is sliced, a can of Indian meal comes to the front, and then they go for the frying-pans.

"Holy Moses! Look here. Just see the ants and bugs."

Second Man.—"Well, I should say! I can see your ants and bugs, and go you an ear wig better."

Third Man (inverting his pan spitefully over the fire).—"D—n 'em, I'll roast the beggars."

Bush D. (who is something of a cook and woodsman)—"Boys, I'll take the pot. I've got a thousand-legged worm at the head of a pismire flush, and it serves us right, for a lot of slovens. Dishes should be cleaned as often as they are used. Now let's scour our pans and commence right."

Hot water, ashes, and soap soon restore the pans to pristine brightness; three frying-pans are filled with trout well rolled in meal; a fourth is used for cooking a can of tomatoes; the coffee is strong, and everything comes out without being smoked or scorched. The trout are browned to a turn, and even the O. W. admits that the dinner is a success. When it is over the dishes are cleaned and put away, and the camp slicked up, there comes the usual two hours of lounging, smoking, and story telling, so dear to the hearts of those who love to go a-fishing and camping. At length there is a lull in the conversation, and Bush D. turns to the old woodsman with, "I thought, 'Uncle Mart,' you were going to show us fellows such a lot of kinks about camping out, camp-fires, cooking, and all that sort of thing, isn't it about time to begin? Strikes me you have spent most of the last twenty-four hours holding down that log."

"Except cutting some night wood and tending the fire," adds number two.

The old woodsman, who has been rather silent up to this time, knocks the ashes leisurely from his pipe, and gets on his feet for a few remarks. He says, "Boys, a bumblebee is biggest when it's first born. You've learned more than you think in the last twenty-four hours."

"Well, as how? Explain yourself," says Bush D.

O. W.—"In the first place, you have learned better than to stick your cooking-kit into a tumbled down heap of knots, mulch and wet bark, only to upset and melt down the pots, and scorch or smoke everything in the pans, until a starving hound wouldn't eat the mess. And you have found that it don't take a log heap to boil a pot of coffee or fry a pan of trout. Also, that a level bed of live coals makes an excellent cooking fire, though I will show you a better. Yesterday you cooked the worst meal I ever saw in the woods. To-day you get up a really good, plain dinner; you have learned that much in one day. Oh, you improve some. And I think you have taken a lesson in cleanliness to-day."

"Yes; but we learned that of the ant—and bug," says number two.

O. W.—"Just so. And did you think all the ants and doodle-bugs blundered into that grease in one morning? I put 'em in myself—to give you a 'kink.'"

Bush D. (disgusted).—"You blasted, dirty old sinner."

Second Man.—"Oh, you miserable old swamp savage; I shan't get over that ear-wig in a month."

Third Man (plaintively).—"This life in the woods isn't what it's cracked up to be; I don't relish bugs and spiders. I wish I were home. I'm all bitten up with punkies, and—

Fourth Man (savagely).—"Dashed old woods-loafer; let's tie his hands and fire him in the creek."

O. W. (placidly).—"Exactly, boys. Your remarks are terse, and to the point. Only, as I am going to show you a trick or two on woodcraft this afternoon, you can afford to wait a little. Now, quit smoking, and get out your hatchets; we'll go to work."

Three hatchets are brought to light; one of them a two-pound clumsy hand-axe, the others of an old time, Mt. Vernon, G. W. pattern. "And now," says good-natured Bush, "you give directions and we'll do the work."

Under directions, the coarse browse of the previous night is placed outside the shanty; three active youngsters, on hands and knees, feel out and cut off every offending stub and root inside the shanty, until it is smooth as a floor. The four small logs are brought to camp; the two longest are laid at the sides and staked in place; the others are placed, one at the head, the other at the foot, also staked; and the camp has acquired definite outlines, and a measurable size of eight by nine feet. Three hemlock logs and two sharpened stakes are toted to camp; the stakes driven firmly, and the logs laid against them, one above the other. Fire-dogs, fore-stick, etc., complete the arrangement, and the camp-fire is in shape for the coming night, precisely as shown in the engraving on page 47.

"And now," says the O. W., "if three of you will go down to the flat and pick the browse clean from the two hemlock tops, Bush and I will fix a cooking-range."

"A—what?" asks one.

"Going to start a boarding-house?" says another.

"Notion of going into the hardware business?" suggests a third.

"Never mind, sonny; just 'tend to that browse, and when you see a smoke raising on the flat by the spring, come over and see the range." And the boys, taking a couple of blankets in which to carry the browse, saunter away to the flat below.

A very leisurely, æsthetic, fragrant occupation is this picking browse. It should never be cut, but pulled, stripped or broken. I have seen a Senator, ex-Governor, and a wealthy banker enjoying themselves hugely at it, varying the occupation by hacking small timber with their G. W. hatchets, like so many boys let loose from school. It may have looked a trifle undignified, but I dare say they found their

G. W. HATCHET.

account in it. Newport or Long Branch would have been more expensive, and much less healthful.

For an hour and a half tongues and fingers are

busy around the hemlock tops; then a thin, long volume of blue smoke rises near the spring, and the boys walk over to inspect the range. They find it made as follows: Two logs six feet long and eight inches thick are laid parallel, but seven inches apart at one end and only four at the other. They are bedded firmly and flattened a little on the inside. On the upper sides the logs are carefully hewed and leveled until pots, pans and kettles will sit firmly and evenly on them. A strong forked stake is driven at each end of the space, and a cross-pole, two or three inches thick, laid on, for hanging kettles. This completes the range; simple, but effective. (See illustration.) The broad end of the space is for frying-pans, and the potato kettle. The narrow end, for coffee-pots and utensils of lesser diameter. From six to eight dishes can be cooked at the same time. Soups, stews, and beans are to be cooked in closely covered kettles hung from the cross-pole, the bottoms of the kettles reaching within some two inches of the logs. With a moderate fire they may be left to simmer for hours without care or attention.

The fire is of the first importance. Start it with fine kindling and clean, dry, hemlock bark. When you have a bright, even fire from end to end of the space, keep it up with small fagots of the sweetest and most wholesome woods in the forest. These are, in the order named, black birch, hickory, sugar maple, yellow birch and red beech. The sticks should be short, and not over two inches across. Split wood is better than round. The out-door range can be made by one man in little more than an hour, and the camper-out, who once tries it, will never wish to see a "portable camp-stove" again.

When the sun leaves the valley in the shade of

OUT-DOOR COOKING RANGE.

Asaph Mountain, the boys have a fragrant bed of elastic browse a foot deep in the shanty, with pillows improvised from stuffed boot legs, cotton handkerchiefs, etc. They cook their suppers on the range, and vote it perfect, no melting or heating handles too hot for use, and no smoking of dishes, or faces.

Just at dark—which means 9 P. M. in the last week of June—the fire is carefully made and chinked. An hour later it is throwing its grateful warmth and light directly into camp, and nowhere else. The camp turns in. Not to wriggle and quarrel with obdurate stubs, but to sleep. And sleep they do. The sound, deep, restful sleep of healthy young manhood, inhaling pure mountain air on the healthiest bed yet known to man.

When it is past midnight, the fire burns low, and the chill night breeze drifts into camp, they still do not rouse up, but only spoon closer, and sleep right on. Only the O. W. turns out sleepily, at two bells in the middle watch, after the manner of hunters, trappers and sailors, the world over. He quietly rebuilds the fire, reduces a bit of navy plug to its lowest denomination, and takes a solitary smoke— still holding down his favorite log. Quizzically and quietly he regards the sleeping youngsters, and wonders if among them all there is one who will do as he has done, *i. e.*, relinquish all of what the world reckons as success, for the love of nature and a free forest life. He hopes not. And yet, as he glances at the calm yellow moon overhead, and listens to the low murmur of the little waterfall below the spring, he has a faint notion that it is not all loss and dross.

Knocking the ashes from his pipe he prepares to turn in, murmuring to himself, half sadly, half humorously, "I have been young, and now I am old; yet have I never seen the true woodsman forsaken, or his seed begging bread—or anything else, so to speak—unless it might be a little tobacco or a nip of whisky." And he creeps into his blanket-bag, backs softly up to the outside man, and joins the snorers.

It is broad daylight when he again turns out, leaving the rest still sleeping soundly. He starts a lively fire in the range, treats two coffee pots to a double handful of coffee and three pints of water each, sets on the potato kettle, washes the potatoes, then sticks his head into the camp, and rouses the party with a regular second mate's hail. "Sta-a-ar-bo'lin's aho-o-o-y. Turn out, you beggars. Come on deck and see it rain." And the boys do turn out. Not with wakeful alacrity, but in a dazed, dreamy, sleepy way. They open wide eyes, when they see that the sun is turning the sombre tops of pines and hemlocks to a soft orange yellow.

"I'd have sworn," says one, "that I hadn't slept over fifteen minutes by the watch."

"And I," says another, "was just watching the fire, when I dropped off in a doze. In about five minutes I opened my eyes, and I'll be shot if it wasn't sunrise."

"As for me," says a third, "I don't know as I've slept at all. I remember seeing somebody poking the fire last night. Next thing I knew, some lunatic was yelling around camp about 'starbolin's,' and 'turning out.' Guess I'll lay down and have my nap out."

"Yes," says the O. W., "I would. If I was a healthy youngster, and couldn't get along with seven hours and a half of solid sleep, I'd take the next forenoon for it.   Just at present, I want to remark that I've got the coffee and potato business under-way, and I'll attend to them.   If you want anything else for breakfast, you'll have to cook it."

And the boys, rising to the occasion, go about the breakfast with willing hands.   It is noticeable, how-ever, that only one pan of trout is cooked, two of the youngsters preferring to fall back on broiled ham, remarking that brook trout is too rich and cloying for a steady diet.   Which is true.   The appetite for trout has very sensibly subsided, and the boyish eagerness for trout fishing has fallen off immensely. Only two of the party show any interest in the riffles. They stroll down stream leisurely, to try their flies for an hour or two.   The others elect to amuse them-selves about camp, cutting small timber with their little hatchets, picking fresh browse, or skirmishing the mountain side for wintergreen berries and sassa-fras.   The fishermen return in a couple of hours, with a score of fair-sized trout.   They remark apolo-getically that it is blazing hot—and there are plenty of trout ahead.   Then they lean their rods against the shanty, and lounge on the blankets, and smoke and doze.

It is less than forty-eight hours since the cross-pole was laid; and, using a little common sense woodcraft, the camp has already attained to a systematic no-system of rest, freedom and idleness.   Every man is free to "loaf, and invite his soul."   There is good trouting within an hour's walk for those who choose, and there is some interest, with a little exercise, in cooking and cutting night wood, slicking up, etc. But the whole party is stricken with "camp-fever," "Indian laziness," the *dolce far niente*. It is over and around every man, enveloping him as with a roseate blanket from the Castle of Indolence.

It is the perfect summer camp.

And it is no myth; but a literal *resume* of a five days' outing at Poplar Spring, on Marsh Creek, in June, 1860. Alas, for the beautiful valley, that once afforded the finest camping grounds I have ever known.

> "Never any more
> Can it be
> Unto me (or anybody else)
> As before."

A huge tannery, six miles above Poplar Spring, poisons and blackens the stream with chemicals, bark and ooze. The land has been brought into market, and every acre eagerly bought up by actual settlers. The once fine covers and thickets are converted into fields thickly dotted with blackened stumps. And, to crown the desolation, heavy laden trains of "The Pine Creek and Jersey Shore R. R." go thundering almost hourly over the very spot where stood our camp by Poplar Spring.

Of course, this is progress; but, whether backward or forward, had better be decided sixty years hence. And, just what has happened to the obscure valley of Marsh Creek, is happening to-day, on a larger scale, all over the land. It is the same old story of grab

4

and greed. Let us go on the "make" to-day, and "whack up" to-morrow; cheating each other as villainously as we may, and posterity be d—d. "What's all the w-u-u-rld to a man when his wife is a widdy?"

This is the *morale:* From Maine to Montana; from the Adirondacks to Alaska; from the Yosemite to the Yellowstone, the trout-hog, the deer-wolf, the netter, the skin-hunter, each and all have it their own way; and the law is a farce—only to be enforced where the game has vanished forever. Perhaps the man-child is born who will live to write the moral of all this—when it is too late.

CHAPTER VII.

MORE HINTS ON COOKING, WITH SOME SIMPLE RE-
CEIPTS.—BREAD, COFFEE, POTATOES, SOUPS,
STEWS, BEANS, FISH, MEAT, VENISON.

"We may live without friends, we may live without books,
But civilized man cannot live without cooks."

IT IS probably true that nothing connected with out-door life in camp is so badly botched as the cooking. It is not through any lack of the raw material, which may be had of excellent quality in any country village. It is not from lack of intelligence or education, for the men you meet in the woods, as outers or sportsmen, are rather over than under the average in these respects. Perhaps it is because it has been dinned into our ears from early childhood, that an appetite, a healthy longing for something good to eat, a tickling of the palate with wholesome, appetizing food, is beneath the attention of an æsthetic, intellectual man. Forgetting that the entire man, mental and physical, depends on proper aliment and the healthy assimilation thereof; and that a thin, dyspeptic man can no more keep up in the struggle of life, than the lightning express can make connections, drawn by a worn out locomotive.

I have never been able to get much help from cook-books, or the scores of receipts published in various works on out-door sport. Take, for example, Frank Forester's "Fish and Fishing." He has more than seventy receipts for cooking fish, over forty of which contain terms or names in French. I dare say they are good—for a first-class hotel. I neither cook or converse in French, and I have come to know that the plainest cooking is the best, so that it be well done and wholesome. In making up the rations for camping out, the first thing usually attended to is bread. And if this be light well-made bread, enough may be taken along to last four or five days, and this may be eked out with Boston crackers, or the best hard-tack, for a couple or three days more, without the least hardship. Also, there are few camps in which some one is not going out to the clearings every few days for mail, small stores, etc., and a supply of bread can be arranged for, with less trouble than it can be made. There are times, however when this is not feasible, and there are men who prefer warm bread all the time. In this case the usual resort, from Maine to Alaska, is the universal flapjack. I do not like it; I seldom make it; it is not good. But it may be eaten, with maple syrup or sugar and butter. I prefer a plain water Johnny-cake, made as follows (supposing your tins are something like those described in Chapter II.): Put a little more than a pint of water in your kettle and bring it to a sharp boil, adding a small teaspoonful of salt, and two of sugar. Stir in slowly enough good corn meal to make a rather stiff mush, let it cook a few minutes, and set it off the fire; then grease your largest tin dish and put the mush in it, smoothing it on top. Set the dish on the out-door range described in the previous chapter, with a lively bed of coals beneath—but no blaze. Invert the second sized tin over the cake, and cover the dish with bright live coals, that bottom and top may bake evenly, and give it from thirty-five to forty minutes for baking. It makes wholesome, palatable bread, which gains on the taste with use.

Those who prefer wheat bread can make a passable article by using the best wheat flour with baking powders, mixing three tablespoonfuls of the powders to a quart of flour. Mix and knead thoroughly with warm water to a rather thin dough, and bake as above. Use the same proportions for pancake batter. When stopping in a permanent camp with plenty of time to cook, excellent light bread may be made by using National yeast cakes, though it is not necessary to "set" the sponge as directed on the papers. Scrape and dissolve half a cake of the yeast in a gill of warm water, and mix it with the flour. Add warm water enough to make it pliable, and not too stiff; set in a warm place until it rises sufficiently, and bake as directed above. It takes several hours to rise.

I am afraid I shall discount my credit on camp cooking when I admit that—if I must use fine flour—I prefer unleavened bread; what my friends irreverently call "club bread." Not that it was ever made or endorsed by any club of men that I know of, but because it is baked on a veritable club, of sassafras or black birch. This is how to make it: Cut a club two feet long and three inches thick at the broadest end; peel or shave off the bark smoothly, and sharpen the smaller end neatly. Then stick the sharpened end in the ground near the fire, leaning the broad end toward a bed of live coals, where it will get screeching hot. While it is heating, mix rather more than a half pint of best Minnesota flour with enough warm water to make a dough. Add a half teaspoonful of salt, and a teaspoonful of sugar, and mould and pull the dough until it becomes lively. Now, work it into a ribbon two inches wide and half an inch thick, wind the ribbon spirally around the broad end of the club, stick the latter in front of the fire so that the bread will bake evenly and quickly to a light brown, and turn frequently until done, which will be in about thirty minutes. When done take it from the fire, stand the club firmly upright, and pick the bread off in pieces as you want it to eat. It will keep hot a long time, and one soon becomes fond of it.

To make perfect coffee, just two ingredients are necessary, and only two. These are water and coffee. It is owing to the bad management of the latter that we drink poor coffee.

There are establishments all over the country that make a business of browning the berry, and sending it out in barrels to the retail grocer. It is all browned too lightly, and, kept loosely in barrels or boxes, it loses what little aroma it ever had, in a few days. We allow the grocer to run it on us, because it saves so much bother, this having our coffee ready browned and ground to our hands. But it is not the way to have good coffee. This can only be had by using the fresh browned, fresh ground berry, and plenty of it; and it must not be of a light brown, as often recommended. To brown it rightly, put a pound of the green berry into a large spider over a hot fire, and stir it constantly until it turns very dark, with a greasy appearance on the surface of the berry. Put it in a tight can at once, if intended for home use, and grind as wanted. If intended for the woods, grind it while hot, and can it tightly.

As for the best berry, Mocha is generally conceded first place, with Java a close second. It is the fashion at present to mix the two in proportions to suit, some taking two parts Java to one of Mocha, others reversing these proportions. Either way is good, or the Mocha is quite as good alone. But there is a better berry than either for the genuine coffee toper. This is the small, dark green berry that comes to market under the generic name of Rio, that name covering half a dozen grades of coffee raised in different provinces of Brazil, throughout a country extending north and south for more than 1,200 miles. The berry alluded to is produced along the range of high hills to the westward of Bahia, and extending north toward the Parnahiba. It has never arrested attention as a distinct grade of the article, but it contains more coffee or caffein to the pound than any berry known to commerce. It is the smallest, heaviest and darkest green of any coffee that comes to our market from Brazil, and may be known by these traits. I have tested it in the land where it is grown, and also at home, for the past sixteen years, and I place it at the head of the list, with Mocha next. Either will make perfect coffee, if treated as follows: Of the berry, browned and ground, as before directed, take six heaping tablespoonfuls, and add three pints of cold water; place the kettle over the fire and bring to a sharp boil; set it a little aside where it will bubble and simmer until wanted, and just before pouring, drip in a half gill of cold water to settle it. That is all there is of it. The quantity of berry is about twice as much as usually given in recipes; but if you want coffee, you had better add two spoonfuls than cut off one.

In 1867, and again in 1870, I had occasion to visit the West India Islands and Brazil. In common with most coffee topers, I had heard much of the super-excellence ascribed to "West India coffee" and "Brazilian coffee.' I concluded to investigate. I had rooms at the Hotel d'Europe, Para, North Brazil. There were six of us, English and American boarders. Every morning, before we were out of our hammocks, a barefooted, half naked Mina negress came around and served each of us with a small cup of strong, black coffee, and sugar *ad libitum.* There was not enough of it for a drink; it was rather in the nature of a medicine, and so intended—"To kill the biscos," they said. The coffee was above criticism.

I went, in the dark of a tropical morning, with Senor Joao, to the coffee factory where they browned the berry, and saw him buy a pound, smoking hot, for which he paid twenty-five cents, or quite as much as it would cost in New York. In ten minutes the coffee was at the hotel, and ground. This is the way they brewed it: A round-bottomed kettle was sitting on the brick range, with a half gallon of boiling water in it. Over the kettle a square piece of white flannel was suspended, caught up at the corners like a dip net. In this the coffee was placed, and a small darky put in his time steadily with a soup ladle, dipping the boiling water from the kettle and pouring it on the coffee. There was a constant stream percolating through coffee and cloth, which, in the course of half an hour, became almost black, and clear as brandy. This was "Brazilian coffee." As the cups used were very small, and as none but the Northerners drank more than one cup, I found that the hotel did not use over two quarts of coffee each morning. It struck me that a pound of fresh Rio coffee berry ought to make a half gallon of rather powerful coffee.

On my arrival home—not having any small darky or any convenient arrangement for the dip net—I had a sack made of light, white flannel, holding about one pint. Into this I put one-quarter pound of freshly ground berry, with water enough for five large cups. It was boiled thoroughly, and proved just as good as the Brazilian article, but too strong for any of the family except the writer. Those who

have a fancy for clear, strong "Brazilian coffee," will
see how easily and simply it can be made.

But, on a heavy knapsack-and-rifle tramp among
the mountains, or a lone canoe cruise in a strange
wilderness, I do not carry coffee. I prefer tea.
Often, when too utterly tired and beaten for further
travel, I have tried coffee, whisky or brandy, and a
long experience convinces me that there is nothing
so restful and refreshing to an exhausted man as a
dish of strong, green tea. To make it as it should
be made, bring the water to a high boil, and let it
continue to boil for a full minute. Set it off the fire
and it will cease boiling; put in a handful of tea,
and it will instantly boil up again; then set it near
the fire, where it will simmer for a few minutes, when
it will be ready for use. Buy the best green tea you
can find, and use it freely on a hard tramp. Black,
or Oolong tea, is excellent in camp. It should be
put in the pot with cold water, brought to the boiling point, and allowed to boil for five minutes.

Almost any man can cook potatoes, but few cook
them well. Most people think them best boiled in
their jackets, and to cook them perfectly in this
manner is so simple and easy, that the wonder is
how any one can fail. A kettle of screeching hot
water with a small handful of salt in it, good potatoes of nearly equal size, washed clean and clipped
at the ends, these are the requisites. Put the potatoes in the boiling water, cover closely, and keep
the water at high boiling pitch until you can thrust
a sharp sliver through the largest potato. Then

drain off the water, and set the kettle in a hot place with the lid partly off. Take them out only as they are wanted; lukewarm potatoes are not good. They will be found about as good as potatoes can be, when cooked in their jackets. But there is a better way, as thus: Select enough for a mess, of smooth, sound tubers; pare them carefully, taking off as little as possible, because the best of the potato lies nearest the skin, and cook as above. When done, pour the water off to the last drop; sprinkle a spoonful of salt and fine cracker crumbs over them; then shake, roll and rattle them in the kettle until the outsides are white and floury. Keep them piping hot until wanted. It is the way to have perfect boiled potatoes.

Many outers are fond of roast potatoes in camp; and they mostly spoil them in the roasting, although there is no better place than the camp-fire in which to do it. To cook them aright, scoop out a basin-like depression under the fore-stick, three or four inches deep, and large enough to hold the tubers when laid side by side; fill it with bright, hard-wood coals, and keep up a strong heat for half an hour or more. Next, clean out the hollow, place the potatoes in it, and cover them with hot sand or ashes, topped with a heap of glowing coals, and keep up all the heat you like. In about forty minutes commence to try them with a sharpened hard-wood sliver; when this will pass through them they are done, and should be raked out at once. Run the sliver through them from end to end, to let the steam escape, and use immediately, as a roast potato quickly becomes soggy and bitter. I will add that, in selecting a supply of potatoes for camp, only the finest and smoothest should be taken.

A man may be a trout-crank, he may have been looking forward for ten weary months to the time when he is to strike the much dreamed of mountain stream, where trout may be taken and eaten without stint. Occasionally—not often—his dream is realized. For two or three days he revels in fly-fishing, and eating brook trout. Then his enthusiasm begins to subside. He talks less of his favorite flies, and hints that wading hour after hour in ice-water gives him cramps in the calves of his legs. Also, he finds that brook trout, eaten for days in succession, pall on the appetite. He hankers for the flesh-pots of the restaurant, and his soul yearns for the bean-pot of home.

Luckily, some one has brought a sack of white beans, and the expert—there is always an expert in camp—is deputed to cook them. He accepts the trust, and proceeds to do it. He puts a quart of dry beans and a liberal chunk of pork in a two-quart kettle, covers the mess with water, and brings it to a rapid boil. Presently the beans begin to swell and lift the lid of the kettle; their conduct is simply demoniacal. They lift up the lid of the kettle, they tumble out over the rim in a way to provoke a saint, and they have scarcely begun to cook. The expert is not to be beaten. As they rise, he spoons them out and throws them away, until half of the best beans being wasted, the rest settle to business. He fills the kettle with water and watches it for an hour. When bean-skins and scum arise he uses the spoon; and when a ring of greasy salt forms around the rim of the kettle, he carefully scrapes it off, but most of it drops back into the pot. When the beans seem cooked to the point of disintegration, he lifts off the kettle, and announces dinner. It is not a success. The larger beans are granulated rather than cooked, while the mealy portion of them has fallen to the bottom of the kettle, and become scorched thereon, and the smaller beans are too hard to be eatable. The liquid, that should be palatable bean soup, is greasy salt water, and the pork is half raw. The party falls back, hungry and disgusted. Even if the mess were well cooked, it is too salt for eating. And why should this be so? Why should any sensible man spend years in acquiring an education that shall fit him for the struggle of life, yet refuse to spend a single day in learning how to cook the food that must sustain the life? It is one of the conundrums no one will ever find out.

There is no article of food more easily carried, and none that contains more nourishment to the pound, than the bean. Limas are usually preferred, but the large white marrow is just as good. It will pay to select them carefully. Keep an eye on grocery stocks, and when you strike a lot of extra large, clean beans, buy twice as many as you need for camp use. Spread them on a table, a quart at a time, and you will be surprised to find how rapidly you can separate the largest and best from the others. Fully one-half will go to the side of largest and finest, and these may be put in a muslin bag, and kept till wanted. Select the expeditionary pork with equal care, buying nothing but thick, solid, "clear," with a pink tinge. Reject that which is white and lardy. With such material, if you cannot lay over Boston baked beans, you had better sweep the cook out of camp

This is how to cook them: Put a pound or a little more of clean pork in the kettle, with water enough to cover it. Let it boil slowly half an hour. In the mean time, wash and parboil one pint of beans. Drain the water from the pork and place the beans around it; add two quarts of water and hang the kettle where it will boil steadily, but not rapidly, for two hours. Pare neatly and thinly five or six medium sized potatoes, and allow them from thirty to forty minutes (according to size and variety), in which to cook. They must be pressed down among the beans so as to be entirely covered. If the beans be fresh and fine they will probably fall to pieces before time is up. This, if they are not allowed to scorch, makes them all the better. If a portion of the pork be left over, it is excellent sliced very thin when cold, and eaten with bread. The above is a dinner for three or four hungry men.

It is usually the case that some of the party prefer baked beans. To have these in perfection, add one gill of raw beans and a piece of pork three inches square to the foregoing proportions. Boil as above, until the beans begin to crack open; then fork out the smaller piece of pork, place it in the center of your largest cooking tin, take beans enough from the kettle to nearly fill the tin, set it over a bright fire on the range, invert the second sized tin for a cover, place live, hard-wood coals on top, and bake precisely as directed for bread—only, when the coals on top become dull and black, brush them off, raise the cover, and take a look. If the beans are getting too dry, add three or four spoonfuls of liquor from the kettle, replace cover and coals, and let them bake until they are of a rich light brown on top. Then serve. It is a good dish. If Boston can beat it, I don't want to lay up anything for old age.

Brown bread and baked beans have a natural connection in the average American mind, and rightly. They supplement each other, even as spring lamb and green peas with our transatlantic cousins. But there is a better recipe for brown bread than is known to the dwellers of the Hub—one that has captured first prizes at country fairs, and won the approval of epicures from Maine to Minnesota; the one that brought honest old Greeley down, on his strictures anent "country bread." And here is the recipe; take it for what it is worth, and try it fairly before condemning it. It is for home use: One quart of sweet milk, one quart of sour, two quarts of Indian meal and one quart of flour, and a cupful of dark, thin Porto Rico molasses. Use one teaspoonful of soda only. Bake in a steady, moderate oven, for four hours. Knead thoroughly before baking.

Soup is, or should be, a leading food element in every woodland camp. I am sorry to say that nothing is, as a rule, more badly botched, while nothing is more easily or simply cooked as it should be. Soup requires time, and a solid basis of the right material. Venison is the basis, and the best material is the bloody part of the deer, where the bullet went through. We used to throw this away; we have learned better. Cut about four pounds of the bloody meat into convenient pieces, and wipe them as clean as possible with leaves or a damp cloth, but don't wash them. Put the meat into a five-quart kettle nearly filled with water, and raise it to a lively boiling pitch. Let it boil for two hours. Have ready a three-tined fork made from a branch of birch or beech, and with this test the meat from time to time; when it parts readily from the bones, slice in a large onion. Pare six large, smooth potatoes, cut five of them into quarters, and drop them into the kettle; scrape the sixth one into the soup for thickening. Season with salt and white pepper to taste.

When, by skirmishing with the wooden fork, you can fish up bones with no meat on them, the soup is cooked, and the kettle may be set aside to cool. Any hungry sportsman can order the next motion. Squirrels—red, black, gray or fox—make nearly as good a soup as venison,* and a better stew. Hares, rabbits, grouse, quail, or even meadow larks and robins, may

---

*I use the word in its American sense, applying it only in connection with the genus *Cervus*. Speaking by the card, the edible flesh of any wild animal is venison.

be used in making soup; but all small game is better in a stew.

To make a stew, proceed for the first two hours precisely as directed for soup; then slice in a couple of good-sized onions and six medium potatoes. When the meat begins to fall from the bones, make a thickening by rubbing three tablespoonfuls of flour and two spoonfuls of melted butter together; thin to the consistence of cream with liquor from the kettle, and drip slowly into the stew, stirring briskly meanwhile. Allow all soups and stews to boil two hours before seasoning, and use only best table salt and white (or black) pepper. Season sparingly; it is easier to put salt in than to get it out. Cayenne pepper adds zest to a soup or stew, but, as some dislike it, let each man season his plate to his own cheek.

Fried squirrels are excellent for a change, but are mostly spoiled by poor cooks, who put tough old he's and tender young squirrels together, treating all alike. To dress and cook them properly, chop off heads, tails and feet with the hatchet; cut the skin on the back crosswise, and, inserting the two middle fingers, pull the skin off in two parts (head and tail). Clean and cut them in halves, leaving two ribs on the hindquarters. Put hind and fore quarters into the kettle, and parboil until tender. This will take about twenty minutes for young ones, and twice as long for the old. When a sharpened sliver will pass easily through the flesh, take the hindquarters from the kettle, drain, and place them in the frying-pan with pork fat hissing hot. Fry to a light, rich brown. It is the only proper way to cook squirrels. The forequarters are to be left in the kettle for a stew.

It sometimes happens that pigeons are very plenty, and the camp is tempted into over-shooting and over-cooking, until every one is thoroughly sick of pigeons. This is all wrong. No party is, or can be, justified in wanton slaughter, just because birds happen to be plenty; they will soon be scarce enough. Pigeons are hardly game, and they are not a first-class bird; but a good deal may be got out of them by the following method: Dress them, at the rate of two birds to one man; save the giblets; place in the kettle, and boil until the sliver will easily pierce the breast; fork them out, cut the thick meat from each side of the breast bone, roll slightly in flour, and put the pieces in the pan, frying them in the same way as directed for squirrels. Put the remainder of the birds in the kettle for a stew.

Quail are good cooked in the same manner, but are better roasted or broiled. To roast them, parboil for fifteen minutes, and in the meantime cut a thin hard-wood stick, eighteen inches, long for each bird. Sharpen the sticks neatly at both ends; impale the birds on one end and thrust the sticks into the ground near the fire, leaning them so that the heat will strike strongly and evenly. Hang a strip of pork between the legs of each bird, and turn frequently until they are a rich brown. When the sharpened sliver will pass easily through the breast they are done.

Woodcock are to be plucked, but not drawn.

Suspend the bird in a bright, clear heat, hang a ribbon of fat pork between the legs, and roast until well done; do not parboil him.

Ruffed grouse are excellent roasted in the same manner, but should first be parboiled. Mallards, teal, butterballs, all edible ducks, are to be treated the same as grouse. If you are ever lucky enough to feast on a canvas-back roasted as above, you will be apt to borrow a leaf from Oliver Twist.

Venison steak should be pounded to tenderness, pressed and worked into shape with the hunting-knife, and broiled over a bed of clean hard-wood coals. A three-pronged birch fork makes the best broiler. For roast venison, the best portion is the forward part of the saddle. Trim off the flanky parts and ends of the ribs; split the backbone lengthwise, that the inner surface may be well exposed; hang it by a strong cord or bark string in a powerful, even heat; lay thin strips of pork along the upper edge, and turn from time to time until done. It had better be left a little rare than overdone. Next to the saddle for roasting, comes the shoulder. Peel this smoothly from the side, using the hunting knife; trim neatly, and cut off the leg at the knee; gash the thickest part of the flesh, and press shreds of pork into the gashes, with two or three thin slices skewered to the upper part. Treat it in the roasting as described above. It is not equal to the saddle when warm, but sliced and eaten cold, is quite as good.

And do not despise the fretful porcupine; he is better than he looks. If you happen on a healthy young specimen when you are needing meat, give him a show before condemning him. Shoot him humanely in the head, and dress him. It is easily done; there are no quills on the belly, and the skin peels as freely as a rabbit's. Take him to camp, parboil him for thirty minutes, and roast or broil him to a rich brown over a bed of glowing coals. He will need no pork to make him juicy, and you will find him very like spring lamb, only better.

I do not accept the decision that ranks the little gray rabbit as a hare, simply because he has a slit in his lip; at all events I shall call him a rabbit for convenience, to distinguish him from his long-legged cousin, who turns white in winter, never takes to a hole, and can keep ahead of hounds nearly all day, affording a game, musical chase that is seldom out of hearing. He never by any chance has an ounce of fat on him, and is not very good eating. He can, however, be worked into a good stew or a passable soup—provided he has not been feeding on laurel. The rabbit is an animal of different habits, and different attributes. When jumped from his form, he is apt to "dig out" for a hole or the nearest stone heap. Sometimes an old one will potter around a thicket, ahead of a slow dog, but his tendency is always to hole. But he affords some sport, and as an article of food, beats the long-legged hare out of sight. He is excellent in stews or soups, while the after half of him, flattened down with the hatchet, parboiled and fried brown in butter or pork fat, is equal to spring chicken.

In cooking fish, as of flesh and fowl, the plainest
and simplest methods are best; and for anything
under two pounds, it is not necessary to go beyond
the frying-pan. Trout of over a pound should be
split down the back, that they may be well in the pan,
and cook evenly. Roll well in meal, or a mixture of
meal and flour, and fry to a rich brown in pork fat,
piping hot. Larger fish may just as well be fried,
but are also adapted to other methods, and there are
people who like fish broiled and buttered, or boiled.
To broil a fish, split him on the back and broil him
four minutes, flesh side down, turn and broil the
other side an equal time. Butter and season to taste.
To boil, the fish should weigh three pounds or more.
Clean, and crimp him by gashing the sides deeply
with a sharp knife. Put him in a kettle of boiling
water strongly salted, and boil twenty-five minutes.
For each additional pound above three, add five
minutes. For gravy, rub together two tablespoonfuls
of flour and one of melted butter, add one heaping
teaspoonful of condensed milk, and thin with liquor
from the kettle. When done, it should have the con
sistence of cream. Take the fish from the kettle,
drain, pour the gravy over it, and eat only with
wheat bread or hard-tack, with butter. The simplest is best, healthiest, and most appetizing.

As a rule, on a mountain tramp or a canoe cruise,
I do not tote canned goods. I carry my duffle in a
light, pliable knapsack, and there is an aggravating
antagonism between the uncompromising rims of a
fruit-can, and the knobs of my vertebræ, that twenty

years of practice has utterly failed to reconcile. And yet, I have found my account in a can of condensed milk, not for tea or coffee, but on bread as a substitute for butter. And I have found a small can of Boston baked beans a most helpful lunch, with a nine-mile carry ahead. It was not epicurean, but had staying qualities.

I often have a call to pilot some muscular young friend into the deep forest, and he usually carries a large pack-basket, with a full supply of quart cans of salmon, tomatoes, peaches, etc. As in duty bound, I admonish him kindly, but firmly, on the folly of loading his young shoulders with such effeminate luxuries; often, I fear, hurting his young feelings by brusque advice. But at night, when the camp-fire burns brightly, and he begins to fish out his tins, the heart of the Old Woodsman relents, and I make amends by allowing him to divide the groceries.

There is a method of cooking usually called "mudding up," which I have found to preserve the flavor and juiciness of ducks, grouse, etc., better than any other mode. I described the method in *Forest and Stream* more than a year ago, but a brief repetition may not be out of place here. Suppose the bird to be cooked is a mallard, or better still, a canvas-back. Cut off the head and most part of the neck; cut off the pinions and pull out the tail feathers, make a plastic cake of clay or tenacious earth an inch thick, and large enough to envelop the bird, and cover him with it snugly. Dig an oval pit under the fore-stick, large enough to hold him, and fill it with hot coals, keeping up a strong heat. Just before turning in for the night, clean out the pit, put in the bird, cover with hot embers and coals, keeping up a brisk fire over it all night. When taken out in the morning you will have an oval, oblong mass of baked clay, with a well roasted bird inside. Let the mass cool until it can be handled, break off the clay, and feathers and skin will come with it, leaving the bird clean and skinless. Season it as you eat, with salt, pepper, and a squeeze of lemon if you like, nothing else.

In selecting salt, choose that which has a gritty feel when rubbed between the thumb and finger, and use white pepper rather than black, grinding the berry yourself. Procure a common tin pepper-box, and fill it with a mixture of fine salt and Cayenne pepper —ten spoonfuls of the former and one of the latter. Have it always where you can lay your hand on it; you will come to use it daily in camp, and if you ever get lost, you will find it of value. Fish and game have a flat, flashy taste eaten without salt, and are also unwholesome.

Do not carry any of the one hundred and one con-diments, sauces, garnishes, etc., laid down in the books. Salt, pepper, and lemons fill the bill in that line. Lobster-sauce, shrimp-sauce, marjoram, celery, parsley, thyme, anchovies, etc., may be left at the hotels.

It may be expected that a pocket volume on wood-craft should contain a liberal chapter of instruction on hunting. It would be quite useless. Hunters, like poets, are born, not made. The art cannot be taught on paper. A few simple hints, however, may not be misplaced. To start aright, have your clothes fitted for hunting. Buy no advertised hunting coats or suits. Select good cassimere of a sort of dull, no-colored, neutral tint, like a decayed stump, and have coat, pants, and cap made of it. For foot-gear, two pairs of heavy yarn socks, with rubber shoes or buck-skin moccasins. In hunting, "silence is gold." Go quietly, slowly, and silently. Remember that the bright-eyed, sharp-eared wood-folk can see, hear and smell, with a keenness that throws your dull faculties quite in the shade. As you go lumbering and stick-breaking through the woods, you will never know how many of these quietly leave your path to right and left, allowing you to pass, while they glide away, unseen, unknown. It is easily seen that a sharp-sensed, light-bodied denizen of the woods can detect the approach of a heavy, bifurcated, booted animal, a long way ahead, and avoid him accordingly.

But there is an art, little known and practiced, that invariably succeeds in outflanking most wild animals; an art, simple in conception and execution, but requiring patience; a species, so to speak, of high art in forestry—the art of "sitting on a log." I could enlarge on this. I might say that the only writer of any note who has mentioned this phase of woodcraft is Mr. Charles D. Warner; and he only speaks of it in painting the character of that lazy old guide, "Old Phelps."

Sitting on a log includes a deal of patience, with oftentimes cold feet and chattering teeth; but, attended to faithfully and patiently, is quite as successful as chasing a deer all day on tracking snow, while it can be practiced when the leaves are dry, and no other mode of still-hunting offers the ghost of a chance. When a man is moving through the woods, wary, watchful animals are pretty certain to catch sight of him. But let him keep perfectly quiet and the conditions are reversed. I have had my best luck, and killed my best deer, by patiently waiting hour after hour on runways. But the time when a hunter could get four or five fair shots in a day by watching a runway has passed away forever. Never any more will buffalo be seen in solid masses covering square miles in one pack. The immense bands of elk and droves of deer are things of the past, and "The game must go."

CHAPTER VIII.

A TEN DAYS' TRIP IN THE WILDERNESS.—GOING IT
ALONE.

ABOUT the only inducements I can think of for
making a ten days' journey through a strange
wilderness, solitary and alone, were a liking for adventure, intense love of nature in her wildest dress,
and a strange fondness for being in deep forests by
myself.

The choice of route was determined by the fact
that two old friends and schoolmates had chosen to
cast their lots in Michigan, one near Saginaw Bay,
the other among the pines of the Muskegon. And
both were a little homesick, and both wrote frequent
letters, in which, knowing my weak point, they exhausted their adjectives and adverbs in describing the
abundance of game and the marvelous fishing. Now,
the Muskegon friend—Davis—was pretty well out of
reach. But Pete Williams, only a few miles out of
Saginaw, was easily accessible. And so it happened,
on a bright October morning, when there came a
frost that cut from Maine to Missouri, that a sudden
fancy took me to use my new Billinghurst on something larger than squirrels. It took about one min-

ute to decide, and an hour to pack such duffle as I needed for a few weeks in the woods.

Remembering Pete's two brown-eyed "kids," and knowing that they were ague-stricken and homesick, I made place for a few apples and peaches, with a ripe melon. For Pete and I had been chums in Rochester, and I had bunked in his attic on Galusha street, for two years. Also, his babies thought as much of me as of their father. The trip to Saginaw was easy and pleasant. A "Redbird" packet to Buffalo, the old propeller Globe to Lower Saginaw, and a ride of half a day on a buckboard, brought me to Pete Williams's clearing. Were they glad to see me? Well, I think so. Pete and his wife cried like children, while the two little homesick "kids" laid their silken heads on my knees and sobbed for very joy. When I brought out the apples and peaches, assuring them that these came from the little garden of their old home—liar that I was—their delight was boundless. And the fact that their favorite tree was a "sour bough," while these were sweet, did not shake their faith in the least.

I staid ten days or more with the Williams family, and the fishing and hunting were all that he had said —all that could be asked. The woods swarmed with pigeons and squirrels; grouse, quail, ducks and wild turkeys were too plenty, while a good hunter could scarcely fail of getting a standing shot at a deer in a morning's hunt. But, *cui bono?* What use could be made of fish or game in such a place? They were all half sick, and had little appetite. Mrs. Williams could not endure the smell of fish; they had been cloyed on small game, and surfeited on venison.

My sporting ardor sank to zero. I had the decency not to slaughter game for the love of killing, and leave it to rot, or hook large fish that could not be used. I soon grew restless, and began to think often about the lumber camp on the Muskegon. By surveyor's lines it was hardly more than sixty miles from Pete Williams's clearing to the Joe Davis camp on the Muskegon. "But practically," said Pete, "Joe and I are a thousand miles apart. White men, as a rule, don't undertake to cross this wilderness. The only one I know who has tried it is old Bill Hance; he can tell you all about it."

Hance was the hunting and trapping genius of Saginaw Bay—a man who dwelt in the woods summer and winter, and never trimmed his hair or wore any other covering on his head. Not a misanthrope, or taciturn, but friendly and talkative rather; liking best to live alone, but fond of tramping across the woods to gossip with neighbors; a very tall man withal, and so thin that, as he went rapidly winding and turning among fallen logs, you looked to see him tangle up and tumble in a loose coil, like a wet rope, but he was better than he looked. He had a high reputation as trailer, guide, or trapper, and was mentioned as a "bad man in a racket." I had met him several times, and as he was decidedly a character, had rather laid myself out to cultivate him. And now that I began to have a strong notion of crossing the woods alone, I took counsel of Bill Hance. Unlike Williams, he thought it perfectly feasible, and rather a neat, gamy thing for a youngster to do. He had crossed the woods several times with surveying parties, and once alone. He knew an Indian trail which led to an old camp within ten miles of the Muskegon, and thought the trail could be followed. It took him a little less than three days to go through; "but," he added, "I nat'rally travel a little faster in the woods than most men. If you can follow the trail, you ought to get through in a little more'n three days—if you keep moggin'."

One afternoon I carefully packed the knapsack and organized for a long woods tramp. I took little stock in that trail, or the three days' notion as to time. I made calculations on losing the trail the first day, and being out a full week. The outfit consisted of rifle, hatchet, compass, blanket-bag, knapsack and knife. For rations, one loaf of bread, two quarts of meal, two pounds of pork, one pound of sugar, with tea, salt, etc., and a supply of jerked venison. One tin dish, twelve rounds of ammunition, and the bullet-molds, filled the list, and did not make a heavy load.

Early on a crisp, bright October morning I kissed the little fellows good-bye, and started out with Hance, who was to put me on the trail. I left the children with sorrow and pity at heart. I am glad now that my visit was a golden hiatus in the sick monotony of their young lives, and that I was able to brighten a few days of their dreary existence. They had begged for the privilege of sleeping with me on a shake-down from the first; and when, as often happened, a pair of little feverish lips would murmur timidly and pleadingly, "I'm so dry; can I have er drink?" I am thankful that I did not put the pleader off with a sip of tepid water, but always brought it from the spring, sparkling and cold. For, a twelvemonth later, there were two little graves in a corner of the stump-blackened garden, and two sore hearts in Pete Williams's cabin.

Hance found the trail easily, but the Indians had been gone a long time, and it was filled with leaves, dim, and not easy to follow. It ended as nearly all trails do; it branched off to right and left, grew dimmer and slimmer, degenerated to a deer path, petered out to a squirrel track, ran up a tree, and ended in a knot hole. I was not sorry. It left me free to follow my nose, my inclinations, and—the compass.

There are men who, on finding themselves alone in a pathless forest, become appalled, almost panic stricken. The vastness of an unbroken wilderness subdues them, and they quail before the relentless, untamed forces of nature. These are the men who grow enthusiastic—at home—about sylvan life, outdoor sports, but always strike camp and come home rather sooner than they intended. And there be some who plunge into an unbroken forest with a feeling of fresh, free, invigorating delight, as they might dash into a crisp ocean surf on a hot day. These know that nature is stern, hard, immovable and terrible in unrelenting cruelty. When wintry winds are

out and the mercury far below zero, she will allow
her most ardent lover to freeze on her snowy breast
without waving a leaf in pity, or offering him a match;
and scores of her devotees may starve to death in as
many different languages before she will offer a loaf
of bread. She does not deal in matches and loaves;
rather in thunderbolts and granite mountains. And
the ashes of her camp-fires bury proud cities. But,
like all tyrants, she yields to force, and gives the
more, the more she is beaten. She may starve or
freeze the poet, the scholar, the scientist; all the
same, she has in store food, fuel and shelter, which
the skillful, self-reliant woodsman can wring from her
savage hand with axe and rifle.

> Only to him whose coat of rags
> Has pressed at night her regal feet,
> Shall come the secrets, strange and sweet,
> Of century pines and beetling crags.

> For him the goddess shall unlock
> The golden secrets which have lain
> Ten thousand years, through frost and rain,
> Deep in the bosom of the rock.

The trip was a long and tiresome one, considering
the distance. There were no hairbreadth escapes; I
was not tackled by bears, treed by wolves, or nearly
killed by a hand-to-claw "racket" with a panther;
and there were no Indians to come sneak-hunting
around after hair. Animal life was abundant, exu-
berant, even. But the bright-eyed woodfolk seemed
tame, nay, almost friendly, and quite intent on mind-
ing their own business. It was a "pigeon year," a

"squirrel year," and also a marvelous year for shack, or mast. Every nut-bearing tree was loaded with sweet, well-filled nuts; and this, coupled with_ the fact that the Indians had left, and the whites had not yet got in, probably accounted for the plenitude of game.

I do not think there was an hour of daylight on the trip when squirrels were not too numerous to be counted, while pigeons were a constant quantity from start to finish. Grouse in the thickets, and quail in the high oak openings, or small prairies, with droves of wild turkeys among heavy timber, were met with almost houriy, and there was scarcely a day on which I could not have had a standing shot at a bear. But the most interesting point about the game was—to me, at least—the marvelous abundance of deer. They were everywhere, on all sorts of ground and among all varieties of timber; very tame they were, too, often stopping to look at the stranger, offering easy shots at short range, and finally going off quite leisurely.

No ardent lover of forest life could be lonely in such company, and in such weather. The only drawback was the harrassing and vexatious manner in which lakes, streams, swamps and marshes constantly persisted in getting across the way, compelling long detours to the north or south, when the true course was nearly due west. I think there were days on which ten hours of pretty faithful tramping did not result in more than three or four miles of direct headway. The headwaters of the Salt and Chippewa rivers were especially obstructive; and, when more than half the distance was covered, I ran into a tangle of small lakes, marshes and swamps, not marked on the map, which cost a hard day's work to leave behind.

While there were no startling adventures, and no danger connected with the trip, there was a constant succession of incident, that made the lonely tramp far from monotonous. Some of these occurrences were intensely interesting, and a little exciting. Perhaps the brief recital of a few may not be uninteresting at the present day, when game is so rapidly disappearing.

My rifle was a neat, hair-triggered Billinghurst, carrying sixty round balls to the pound, a muzzle-loader, of course, and a nail-driver. I made just three shots in ten days, and each shot stood for a plump young deer in the "short blue." It seemed wicked to murder such a bright, graceful animal, when no more than the loins and a couple of slices from the ham could be used, leaving the balance to the wolves, who never failed to take possession before I was out of ear shot. But I condoned the excess, if excess it were, by the many chances I allowed to pass, not only on deer but bear, and once on a big brute of a wild hog, the wickedest and most formidable looking animal I ever met in the woods. The meeting happened in this wise. I had been bothered and wearied for half a day by a bad piece of low, marshy ground, and had at length struck a dry, rolling oak opening, where I sat down at the root of a small oak to rest.

5

I had scarcely been resting ten minutes, when I caught sight of a large, dirty-white animal, slowly working its way in my direction through the low bushes, evidently nosing around for acorns. I was puzzled to say what it was. It looked like a hog, but stood too high on its legs; and how would such a beast get there anyhow? Nearer and nearer he came, and at last walked out into an open spot less than twenty yards distant. It was a wild hog of the ugliest and largest description; tall as a yearling, with an unnaturally large head, and dangerous looking tusks, that curved above his savage snout like small horns. There was promise of magnificent power in his immense shoulders, while flanks and hams were disproportionately light. He came out to the open leisurely munching his acorns, or amusing himself by ploughing deep furrows with his nose, and not until within ten yards did he appear to note the presence of a stranger. Suddenly he raised his head and became rigid as though frozen to stone; he was taking an observation. For a few seconds he remained immovable, then his bristles became erect, and with a deep, guttural, grunting noise, he commenced hitching himself along in my direction, sidewise. My hair raised, and in an instant I was on my feet with the cocked rifle to my shoulder—meaning to shoot before his charge, and then make good time up the tree. But there was no need. As I sprang to my feet he sprang for the hazel bushes, and went tearing through them with the speed of a deer, keeping up a succession of snorts and grunts that could be heard

long after he had passed out of sight. I am not subject to buck fever, and was disgusted to find myself so
badly "rattled" that I could scarcely handle the
rifle. At first I was provoked at myself for not getting a good ready and shooting him in the head, as
he came out of the bushes; but it was better to let
him live. He was not carnivorous, or a beast of
prey, and ugly as he was, certainly looked better
alive than he would as a porcine corpse. No doubt
he relished his acorns as well as though he had been
less ugly, and he was a savage power in the forest.
Bears love pork, even as a darky loves 'possum; and
the fact that he was picking up a comfortable living
in that wilderness, is presumptive evidence that he
was a match for the largest bear, or he would have
been eaten long before.

Another little incident, in which bruin played a
leading part, rises vividly to memory. It was hardly
an adventure; only the meeting of man and bear,
and they parted on good terms, with no hardness on
either side.

The meeting occurred, as usually was the case
with large game, on dry, oak lands, where the under-
growth was hazel, sassafras, and wild grapevine. As
before, I had paused for a rest, when I began to catch
glimpses of a very black animal working its way
among the hazel bushes, under the scattering oaks,
and toward me. With no definite intention of shooting, but just to see how easy it might be to kill him,
I got a good ready, and waited. Slowly and lazily
he nuzzled his way among the trees, sitting up occa-

sionally to crunch acorns, until he was within twenty-five yards of me, with the bright bead neatly showing at the butt of his ear, and he sitting on his haunches, calmly chewing his acorns, oblivious of danger. He was the shortest-legged, blackest, and glossiest bear I had ever seen; and such a fair shot. But I could not use either skin or meat, and he was a splendid picture just as he sat. Shot down and left to taint the blessed air, he would not look as wholesome, let alone that it would be unwarrantable murder. And so, when he came nosing under the very tree where I was sitting, I suddenly jumped up, threw my hat at him, and gave a Comanche yell. He tumbled over in a limp heap, grunting and whining for very terror, gathered himself up, got up headway, and disappeared with wonderful speed—considering the length of his legs.

On another occasion—and this was in heavy timber—I was resting on a log, partially concealed by spice bushes, when I noticed a large flock of turkeys coming in my direction. As they rapidly advanced with their quick, gliding walk, the flock grew to a drove, the drove became a swarm—an army. To right and on the left, as far as I could see in front, a legion of turkeys were marching, steadily marching to the eastward. Among them were some of the grandest gobblers I had ever seen, and one magnificent fellow came straight toward me. Never before or since have I seen such a splendid wild bird. His thick, glossy black beard nearly reached the ground, his bronze uniform was of the richest, and he was decidedly the largest I have ever seen. When within fifty feet of the spot where I was nearly hidden, his wary eye caught something suspicious; and he raised his superb head for an instant in an attitude of motionless attention. Then, with lowered head and drooping tail, he turned right about, gave the note of alarm, put the trunk of a large tree quickly between himself and the enemy, and went away like the wind. With the speed of thought the warning note was sounded along the whole line, and in a moment the woods seemed alive with turkeys, running for dear life. In less time than it takes to tell it, that gallinaceous army had passed out of sight, forever. And the like of it will never again be possible on this continent.

And again, on the morning of the sixth day out, I blundered on to such an aggregation of deer as a man sees but once in a lifetime. I had camped over night on low land, among heavy timber, but soon after striking camp, came to a place where the timber was scattering, and the land had a gentle rise to the westward. Scarcely had I left the low land behind, when a few deer got out of their beds and commenced lazily bounding away. They were soon joined by others; on the right flank, on the left, and ahead, they continued to rise and canter off leisurely, stopping at a distance of one or two hundred yards to look back. It struck me finally that I had started something rather unusual, and I began counting the deer in sight. It was useless to attempt it; their white flags were flying in front and on both flanks, as far as one could see, and new ones seemed constantly joining the procession. Among them were several very large bucks with superb antlers, and these seemed very little afraid of the small, quiet biped in leaf-colored rig. They often paused to gaze back with bold, fearless front, as though inclined to call a halt and face the music; but when within a hundred yards, would turn and canter leisurely away. As the herd neared the summit of the low-lying ridge, I tried to make a reasonable guess at their numbers, by counting a part and estimating the rest, but could come to no satisfactory conclusion. As they passed the summit and loped down the gentle decline toward heavy timber, they began to scatter, and soon not a flag was in sight. It was a magnificent cervine army with white banners, and I shall never look upon its like again. The largest drove of deer I have seen in twenty years consisted of seven only.

And with much of interest, much of tramping, and not a little of vexatious delay, I came at length to a stream that I knew must be the south branch of the Muskegon. The main river could scarcely be more than ten miles to the westward, and might be easily reached in one day.

It was time. The meal and pork were nearly gone, sugar and tea were at low ebb, and I was tired of venison; tired anyhow; ready for human speech and human companionship.

It was in the afternoon of the ninth day that I crossed the South Muskegon and laid a course west by north. The traveling was not bad; and in less than an hour I ran on to the ruins of a camp that I knew to be the work of Indians. It had evidently been a permanent winter camp, and was almost certainly the Indian camp spoken of by Bill Hance. Pausing a short time to look over the ruins, with the lonely feeling always induced by a decayed, rotting camp, I struck due west and made several miles before sundown.

I camped on a little rill, near a huge dry stub that would peel, made the last of the meal into a johnny-cake, broiled the last slice of pork, and laid down with the notion that a ten days' tramp, where it took an average of fifteen miles to make six, ought to end on the morrow. At sunrise I was again on foot, and after three hours of steady tramping, saw a smoky opening ahead. In five minutes I was standing on the left bank of the Muskegon.

And the Joe Davis camp—was it up stream or down? I decided on the latter, and started slowly down stream, keeping an eye out for signs. In less than an hour I struck a dim log road which led to the river, and there was a "landing," with the usual debris of skids, loose bark, chocks, and some pieces of broken boards. It did not take long to construct an efficient dog raft from the dry skids, and as I drifted placidly down the deep, wild river, munching the last bit of johnny-cake, I inwardly swore that my next wilderness cruise should be by water.

It was in late afternoon that I heard—blessed sound—the eager clank, clank, clank of the old-fashioned sawmill. It grew nearer and more distinct; presently I could distinguish the rumble of machinery as the carriage gigged back; then the raft rounded a gentle bend, and a mill, with its long, log boarding-house, came in full sight.

As the raft swung into the landing the mill became silent; a brown-bearded, red-shirted fellow came down to welcome me, a pair of strong hands grasped both my own, and the voice of Joe Davis said earnestly, "Why, George! I never was so d—d glad to see a man in my life!"

The ten days' tramp was ended. It had been wearisome to a degree, but interesting and instructive. I had seen more game birds and animals in the time than I ever saw before or since in a whole season; and, though I came out with clothes pretty well worn and torn off my back and legs, was a little disposed to plume myself on the achievement. Even at this day I am a little proud of the fact that, with so many temptations to slaughter, I only fired three shots on the route. Nothing but the exceptionally fine, dry weather rendered such a trip possible in a wilderness so cut up with swamps, lakes, marshes and streams. A week of steady rain or a premature snow storm—either likely enough at that season— would have been most disastrous; while a forest fire like that of '56, and later ones, would simply have proved fatal.

Reader, if ever you are tempted to make a similar thoughtless, reckless trip—don't do it.

CHAPTER IX.—CANOEING.

> Beneath a hemlock grim and dark,
>   Where shrub and vine are intertwining,
> Our shanty stands, well roofed with bark,
>   On which the cheerful blaze is shining.
> The smoke ascends in spiral wreath.
>   With upward curve the sparks are trending;
> The coffee kettle sings beneath
>   Where sparks and smoke with leaves are blending
>
> And on the stream a light canoe
>   Floats like a freshly fallen feather.
> A fairy thing, that will not do
>   For broader seas and stormy weather.
> Her sides no thicker than the shell
>   Of Ole Bull's Cremona fiddle,
> The man who rides her will do well
>   To part his scalp-lock in the middle.

THE canoe is coming to the front, and canoeing is gaining rapidly in popular favor, in spite of the disparaging remark that "a canoe is the poor man's yacht." The canoe editor of *Forest and Stream* pertinently says, "we may as properly call a bicycle 'the poor man's express train.'" But, suppose it is the poor man's yacht? Are we to be debarred from aquatic sports because we are not rich? And are we such weak flunkies as to be ashamed of poverty? Or to attempt shams and subterfuges to hide it? For myself, I freely accept the imputation. In common with nine-tenths of my fellow citizens I am poor—and the canoe is my yacht, as it would be were I a millionaire. We are a nation of 50,000,000, and comparatively few of us are rich enough to support a yacht, let alone the fact that not one man in fifty lives near enough to yachting waters to make such an acquisition desirable—or feasible, even. It is different with the canoe. A man like myself may live in the backwoods, a hundred miles from a decent sized inland lake, and much further from the sea coast, and yet be an enthusiastic canoeist. For instance.

Last July I made my preparations for a canoe cruise, and spun out with as little delay as possible. I had pitched on the Adirondacks as a cruising ground, and had more than 250 miles of railroads and buckboards to take, before launching the canoe on Moose River. She was carried thirteen miles over the Brown's Tract road on the head of her skipper, cruised from the western side of the Wilderness to the Lower St. Regis on the east side, cruised back again by a somewhat different route, was taken home to Pennsylvania on the cars, 250 miles, sent back to her builder, St. Lawrence county, N. Y., over 300 miles, thence by rail to New York City, where, the last I heard of her, she was on exhibition at the *Forest and Stream* office. She took her chances in the baggage car, with no special care, and is to-day, so far as I know, staunch and tight, with not a check in her frail siding.

Such cruising can only be made in a very light canoe, and with a very light outfit. It was sometimes necessary to make several carries in one day, aggregating as much as ten miles, besides from fifteen to twenty miles under paddle. No heavy, decked, paddling or sailing canoe would have been available for such a trip with a man of ordinary muscle.

The difference between a lone, independent cruise through an almost unbroken wilderness, and cruising along civilized routes, where the canoeist can interview farm houses and village groceries for supplies, getting gratuitous stonings from the small boy, and much reviling from ye ancient mariner of the towpath—I say, the difference is just immense. Whence it comes that I always prefer a very light, open canoe; one that I can carry almost as easily as my hat, and yet that will float me easily, buoyantly, and safely. And such a canoe was my last cruiser. She only weighed ten and one-half pounds when first launched, and after an all-summer rattling by land and water had only gained half a pound. I do not therefore advise any one to buy a ten and a half pound canoe; although she would prove competent for a skillful light weight. She was built to order, as a test of lightness, and was the third experiment in that line.

I have nothing to say against the really fine canoes

that are in highest favor to-day. Were I fond of sailing, and satisfied to cruise on routes where clearings are more plenty than carries, I dare say I should run a Shadow, or Stella Maris, at a cost of considerably more than $100—though I should hardly call it a "poor man's yacht."

Much is being said and written at the present day as to the "perfect canoe." One writer decides in favor of a Pearl 15x31½ inches. In the same column another says, "the perfect canoe does not exist." I should rather say there are several types of the modern canoe, each nearly perfect in its way and for the use to which it is best adapted. The perfect paddling canoe is by no means perfect under canvas, and *vice versa.* The best cruiser is not a perfect racer, while neither of them is at all perfect as a paddling cruiser where much carrying is to be done. And the most perfect canoe for fishing and gunning around shallow, marshy waters, would be a very imperfect canoe for a rough and ready cruise of one hundred miles through a strange wilderness, where a day's cruise will sometimes include a dozen miles of carrying.

Believing, as I do, that the light, single canoe with double-bladed paddle is bound to soon become a leading—if not the leading—feature in summer recreation, and having been a light canoeist for nearly fifty years, during the last twenty of which I experimented much with the view of reducing weight perhaps I can give some hints that may help a younger man in the selection of a canoe which shall be safe, pleasant to ride, and not burdensome to carry.

Let me premise that, up to four years ago, I was never able to get a canoe that entirely satisfied me as to weight and model. I bought the smallest birches I could find; procured a tiny Chippewa dugout from North Michigan, and once owned a kyak. They were all too heavy, and they were cranky to a degree.

About twenty years ago I commenced making my own canoes. The construction was of the simplest; a 22-inch pine board for the bottom, planed to ¾ of an inch thickness; two wide ½-inch boards for the sides, and two light oak stems; five pieces of wood in all. I found that the bend of the siding gave too much shear; for instance, if the siding was 12 inches wide, she would have a rise of 12 inches at stems and less than 5 inches at center. But the flat bottom made her very stiff, and for river work she was better than anything I had yet tried. She was too heavy, however, always weighing from 45 to 50 pounds, and awkward to carry.

My last canoe of this style went down the Susquehanna with an ice jam in the spring of '79, and in the meantime canoeing began to loom up. The best paper in the country which makes out-door sport a specialty, devoted liberal space to canoeing, and skilled boatbuilders were advertising canoes of various models and widely different material. I commenced interviewing the builders by letter, and studying catalogues carefully. There was a wide

margin of choice.   You could have lapstreak, smooth
skin, paper, veneer, or canvas.   What I wanted was
light weight, and good model.   I liked the Peterboro
canoes; they were decidedly canoey.   Also, the
veneered Racines; but neither of them talked of a
20-pound canoe. The "Osgood folding canvas" did.
But I had some knowledge of canvas boats.   I knew
they could make her down to 20 pounds.   How
much would she weigh after being in the water a
week, and how would she behave when swamped in
the middle of a lake, were questions to be asked, for
I always get swamped.   One builder of cedar canoes
thought he could make me the boat I wanted, inside
of 20 pounds, clinker-built, and at my own risk, as
he hardly believed in so light a boat.   I sent him
the order, and he turned out what is pretty well
known in "Brown's Tract" as the "Nessmuk canoe."
She weighed just 17 pounds 13¾ ounces, and was
thought to be the lightest working canoe in existence.
Her builder gave me some advice about stiffening
her with braces, etc., if I found her too frail, "and
he never expected to build another like her."

"He builded better than he knew."   She needed
no bracing; and she was, and is, a staunch, sea-
worthy little model.   I fell in love with her from the
start.   I had at last found the canoe that I could
ride in rough water, sleep in afloat, and carry with
ease for miles.   I paddled her early and late, mainly
on the Fulton Chain; but I also cruised her on
Raquette Lake, Eagle, Utowana, Blue Mountain,
and Forked lakes.   I paddled her until there were

black and blue streaks along the muscles from wrist to elbow. Thank Heaven, I had found something that made me a boy again. Her log shows a cruise for 1880 of over 550 miles. .

As regards her capacity (she is now on Third Lake, Brown's Tract), James P. Fifield, a muscular young Forge House guide of 6 feet 2 inches and 185 pounds weight, took her through the Fulton Chain to Raquette Lake last summer; and, happening on his camp, Seventh Lake, last July, I asked him how she performed under his weight. He said, "I never made the trip to the Raquette so lightly and easily in my life." And as to the present opinion of her builder, Mr. Rushton, of Canton, N. Y. He writes me, under date of Nov. 18, '83: "I thought when I built the Nessmuk, no one else would ever want one. But I now build about a dozen of them a year. Great big men, ladies, and two, aye, three schoolboys ride in them. It is wonderful how few pounds of cedar, rightly modeled and properly put together, it takes to float a man." Just so, Mr. Rushton. That's what I said when I ordered her. But few seemed to see it then.

The Nessmuk was by no means the ultimatum of lightness, and I ordered another, six inches longer, two inches wider, and to weigh about 15 pounds. When she came to hand she was a beauty, finished in oil and shellac. But she weighed 16 pounds, and would not only carry me and my duffle, but I could easily carry a passenger of my weight. I cruised her in the summer of '81 over the Fulton Chain,

Raquette Lake, Forked Lake, down the Raquette River, and on Long Lake. But her log only showed a record of 206 miles. The cruise that had been mapped for 600 miles was cut short by sickness, and I went into quarantine at the hostelry of Mitchell Sabattis. Slowly and feebly I crept back to the Fulton Chain, hung up at the Forge House, and the cruise of the Susan Nipper was ended. Later in the season, I sent for her, and she was forwarded by express, coming out over the fearful Brown's Tract road to Boonville (25½ miles) by buckboard. From Boonville home, she took her chances in the baggage car without protection, and reached her destination without a check or scratch. She hangs in her slings under the porch, a thing of beauty—and, like many beauties, a trifle frail—but staunch as the day I took her. Her proper lading is about 200 pounds. She can float 300 pounds.

Of my last and lightest venture, the Sairy Gamp, little more need be said. I will only add that a Mr. Dutton, of Philadelphia, got into her at the Forge House, and paddled her like an old canoeist, though it was his first experience with the double blade. He gave his age as sixty-four years, and weight, 140 pounds. Billy Cornell, a bright young guide, cruised her on Raquette Lake quite as well as her owner could do it, and I thought she trimmed better with him. He paddled at 141½ pounds, which is just about her right lading. And she was only an experiment, anyhow. I wanted to find out how light a canoe it took to drown her skipper, and I do not yet know. I never shall. But, most of all, I desired to settle the question—approximately at least—of weight, as regards canoe and canoeist.

Many years ago, I became convinced that we were all, as canoeists, carrying and paddling just twice as much wood as was at all needful, and something more than a year since, I advanced the opinion in *Forest and Stream*, that ten pounds of well made cedar ought to carry one hundred pounds of man. The past season has more than proved it; but, as I may be a little exceptional, I leave myself out of the question, and have ordered my next canoe on lines and dimensions that, in my judgment, will be found nearly perfect for the average canoeist of 150 to 160 pounds. She will be much stronger than either of my other canoes, because few men would like a canoe so frail and limber that she can be sprung inward by hand pressure on the gunwales, as easily as a hat-box. And many men are clumsy or careless with a boat, while others are lubberly by nature. Her dimensions are: Length, 10½ feet; beam, 26 inches; rise at center, 9 inches; at stems, 15 inches; oval red elm ribs, 1 inch apart; an inch home tumble; stems, plumb and sharp; oak keel and keelson; clinker-built, of white cedar.

Such a canoe will weigh about 22 pounds, and will do just as well for the man of 140 or 170 pounds, while even a light weight of 110 pounds ought to take her over a portage with a light, elastic carrying frame, without distress. She will trim best, however, at about 160 pounds. For a welter, say of some 200 pounds, add 6 inches to her length, 2 inches to her beam, and 1 inch to rise at center. The light weight canoeist will do well to order either of the two canoes advertised in Rushton's catalogue for '84 as Nos. 161 and 162. The first is 10 feet in length; weight, 16 pounds. The other, 10½ feet length, weight, 18 pounds. Either is capable of 160 pounds, and they are very steady and buoyant, as I happen to know. I dare say other manufacturers are building similar boats, but I do not know it.

Provide your canoe with a flooring of oilcloth 3½ feet long by 15 inches wide; punch holes in it and tie it neatly to the ribbing, just where it will best protect the bottom from wear and danger. Use only a cushion for seat, and do not buy a fancy one with permanent stuffing, but get sixpence worth of good, unbleached cotton cloth, and have it sewed into bag shape. Stuff the bag with fine browse, dry grass or leaves, settle it well together, and fasten the open end by turning it flatly back and using two or three pins. You can empty it if you like when going over a carry, and it makes a good pillow at night.

Select a canoe that fits you, just as you would a coat or hat. A 16-pound canoe may fit me exactly, but would be a bad misfit for a man of 180 pounds. And don't neglect the auxiliary paddle, or "pudding stick," as my friends call it. The notion may be new to most canoeists, but will be found exceedingly handy and useful. It is simply a little one-handed paddle weighing 5 to 7 ounces, 20 to 22 inches long, with a blade 3½ inches wide. Work it out of half-inch cherry or maple, and fine the blade down thin. Tie it to a rib with a slip-knot, having the handle in easy reach, and when you come to a narrow, tortuous channel, where shrubs and weeds crowd you on both sides, take the double-blade inboard, use the pudding stick, and you can go almost anywhere that a musk-rat can.

In fishing for trout or floating deer, remember you are dealing with the wary, and that the broad blades are very showy when in motion. Therefore, on approaching a spring-hole, lay the double-blade on the lily-pads where you can pick it up when wanted, and handle your canoe with the auxiliary. On hooking a large fish, handle the rod with one hand and with the other lay the canoe out into deep water, away from all entangling alliances. You may be surprised to find how easily, with a little practice, you can make a two-pound trout or bass tow the canoe the way you want it to go.

In floating for deer, use the double-blade only in making the passage to the ground; then take it apart and lay it inboard, using only the little paddle to float with, tying it to a rib with a yard and a half of linen line. On approaching a deer near enough to shoot, let go the paddle, leaving it to drift alongside while you attend to venison.

CHAPTER X.

ODDS AND ENDS.—WHERE TO GO FOR AN OUTING.
WHY A CLINKER?—BOUGHS AND BROWSE.

THE oft-recurring question as to where to go for
the outing, can hardly be answered at all satisfactorily.   In a general way, any place may, and
ought to be, satisfactory, where there are fresh green
woods, pleasant scenery, and fish and game plenty
enough to supply the camp abundantly, with boating
facilities and pure water.

"It's more in the man than it is in the land,"

and there are thousands of such places on the waters
of the Susquehanna, the Delaware, the rivers and
lakes of Maine, Michigan, Wisconsin, and Canada.

Among the lakes of Central New York one may
easily select a camping ground, healthy, pleasant,
easily reached, and with the advantage of cheapness.
A little too much civilization, perhaps; but the far-
mers are friendly, and kindly disposed to all summer
outers who behave like gentlemen.

For fine forest scenery and unequaled canoeing
facilities, it must be admitted that the Adirondack
region stands at the head.   There is also fine fishing
and good hunting, for those who know the right

places to go for deer and trout. But it is a tedious, expensive job getting into the heart of the Wilderness, and it is the most costly woodland resort I know of when you are there. Without a guide you will be likely to see very little sport, and the guide's wage is $3 per day and board, the latter ranging from $1 to $2 per day; and your own bills at the forest hotels will run from $2 to $4 per day. At the Prospect House, Blue Mountain Lake, they will charge you $25 per week, and your guide half price. On the whole, if you hire a guide and make the tour of the Northern Wilderness as a "gentleman," you will do well to get off for $50 per week. You can reduce this nearly one-half and have much better sport, by going into camp at once, and staying there. The better way is for two men to hire a guide, live in camp altogether, and divide the expense. In this way it is easy to bring the weekly expense within $15 each; and if one can afford it, the money will be well spent.

All along the Alleghany range, from Maine to Michigan, and from Pennsylvania to the Provinces, numberless resorts exist as pleasant, as healthy, as prolific of sport, as the famed Adirondacks, and at half the cost. But, for an all-summer canoe cruise, with more than 600 accessible lakes and ponds, the Northern Wilderness stands alone. And, as a wealthy cockney once remarked to me in Brown's Tract, "It's no place for a poor man."

And now I will give my reasons for preferring the clinker-built cedar boat, or canoe, to any other. First, as to material. Cedar is stronger, more elastic, more enduring, and shrinks less than pine or any other light wood used as boat siding. As one of the best builders in the country says, "It has been thoroughly demonstrated that a cedar canoe will stand more hard knocks than an oak one; for where it only receives bruises, the oak streaks will split." And he might add, the pine will break. But I suppose it is settled beyond dispute that white cedar stands at the head for boat streaks. I prefer it, then, because it is the best. And I prefer the clinker, because it is the strongest, simplest, most enduring, and most easily repaired in case of accident. To prove the strength theory, take a cedar (or pine) strip eight feet long and six inches wide. Bend it to a certain point by an equal strain on each end, and carefully note the result. Next, strip it lengthwise with the rip saw, lap the two halves an inch, and nail the lap as in boat building. Test it again, and you will find it has gained in strength about twenty per cent. That is the clinker of it.

Now work the laps down until the strip is of uniform thickness its entire length, and test it once more; you will find it much weaker than on first trial. That is the smooth skin, sometimes called lapstreak. They, the clinker canoes, are easily tightened when they spring a leak through being rattled over stones in rapids. It is only to hunt a smooth pebble for a clinch head, and settle the nails that have started with the hatchet, putting in a few new ones if needed. And they are put together, at least by the best builders, without any cement or white lead, naked wood to wood, and depending only on close work for water-proofing. And each pair of strips is cut to fit and lie in its proper place without strain, no two pairs being alike, but each pair, from garboards to upper streak, having easy, natural form for its destined position.

The veneered canoes are very fine, for deep water; but a few cuts on sharp stones will be found ruinous; and if exposed much to weather they are liable to warp. The builders understand this, and plainly say that they prefer not to build fine boats for those who will neglect the proper care of them.

The paper boat, also, will not stand much cutting on sharp stones, and is not buoyant when swamped, unless fitted with water-tight compartments, which I abhor.

The canvas is rather a logy, limp sort of craft, to my thinking, and liable to drown her crew if swamped.

But each and all have their admirers, and purchasers as well, while each is good in its way, and I only mention a few reasons for my preference of the cedar.

When running an ugly rapid or crossing a stormy lake, I like to feel that I have enough light, seasoned wood under me to keep my mouth and nose above water all day, besides saving the rifle and knapsack, which, when running into danger, I always tie to the ribbing with strong linen line, as I do the paddle also, giving it about line enough to just allow free play.

I am not—to use a little modern slang—going to "give myself away" on canoeing, or talk of startling adventure. But, for the possible advantage of some future canoeist, I will briefly relate what happened to me on a certain morning in August, 1883. It was on one of the larger lakes—no matter which—between Paul Smith's and the Fulton Chain. I had camped over night in a spot that did not suit me in the least, but it seemed the best I could do then and there. The night was rough, and the early morning threatening. However, I managed a cup of coffee, "tied in," and made a slippery carry of two miles a little after sunrise. Arrived on the shore of the lake, things did not look promising. The whirling, twirling clouds were black and dangerous looking, the crisp, dark waves were crested with spume, and I had a notion of just making a comfortable camp and waiting for better weather. But the commissary department was reduced to six Boston crackers, with a single slice of pork, and it was twelve miles of wilderness to the nearest point of supplies, four miles of it carries, included. Such weather might last a week, and I decided to go. For half an hour I sat on the beach, taking weather notes. The wind was northeast; my course was due west, giving me four points free. Taking five feet of strong line, I tied one end under a rib next the keelson, and the other around the paddle. Stripping to shirt and drawers, I stowed everything in the knapsack, and tied that safely in the fore peak. Then I swung out. Before I was a half mile out, I fervently wished myself back.

But it was too late. How that little, corky, light canoe did bound and snap, with a constant tendency to come up in the wind's eye, that kept me on the *qui vive* every instant. She shipped no water, she was too buoyant for that. But she was all the time in danger of pitching her crew overboard. It soon came to a crisis. About the middle of the lake, on the north side, there is a sharp, low gulch that runs away back through the hills, looking like a level cut through a railroad embankment. And down this gulch came a fierce thunder gust that was like a small cyclone. It knocked down trees, swept over the lake, and—caught the little canoe on the crest of a wave, right under the garboard streak. I went overboard like a shot; but I kept my grip on the paddle. That grip was worth a thousand dollars to the "Travelers Accidental;" and another thousand to the "Equitable Company," because the paddle, with its line, enabled me to keep the canoe in hand, and prevent her from going away to leeward like a dry leaf. When I once got my nose above water, and my hand on her after stem, I knew I had the whole business under control. Pressing the stem down, I took a look inboard. The little jilt! She had not shipped a quart of water. And there was the knapsack, the rod, the little auxiliary paddle, all just as I had tied them in; only the crew and the double-blade had gone overboard. As I am elderly and out of practice in the swimming line, and it was nearly half a mile to a lee shore, and, as I was out of breath and water-logged, it is quite possible that a little forethought and four cents' worth of fishline saved—the insurance companies two thousand dollars.

How I slowly kicked that canoe ashore; how the sun came out bright and hot; how, instead of making the remaining eleven miles, I raised a conflagration and a comfortable camp, dried out, and had a pleasant night of it; all this is neither here nor there. The point I wish to make is, keep your duffle safe to float, and your paddle and canoe sufficiently in hand to always hold your breathing works above water level. So shall your children look confidently for your safe return, while the "Accidentals" arise and call you a good investment.

There is only one objection to the clinker-built canoe that occurs to me as at all plausible. This is, that the ridge-like projections of her, clinker laps offer resistance to the water, and retard her speed. Theoretically, this is correct. Practically, it is not proven. Her streaks are so nearly on her water line that the resistance, if any, must be infinitesimal. It is possible, however, that this element might lessen her speed one or two minutes in a mile race. I am not racing, but taking leisurely recreation. I can wait two or three minutes as well as not. Three or four knots an hour will take me through to the last carry quite as soon as I care to make the landing.

A few words of explanation and advice may not be out of place. I have used the words "boughs" and "browse" quite frequently I am sorry they are not more in use. The first settlers in the unbroken forest knew how to diagnose a tree. They came to the "Holland Purchase" from the Eastern States, with their families, in a covered wagon, drawn by a yoke of oxen, and the favorite cow patiently leading behind. They could not start until the ground was settled, some time in May, and nothing could be done in late summer, save to erect a log cabin, and clear a few acres for the next season. To this end the oxen were indispensable, and a cow was of first necessity, where there were children. And cows and oxen must have hay. But there was not a ton of hay in the country. A few hundred pounds of coarse wild grass was gleaned from the margins of streams and small marshes; but the main reliance was "browse." Through the warm months the cattle could take care of themselves ; but, when winter settled down in earnest, a large part of the settler's work consisted in providing browse for his cattle. First and best was the basswood (linden); then came maple, beech, birch and hemlock. Some of the trees would be nearly three feet in diameter, and, when felled, much of the browse would be twenty feet above the reach of cattle, on the ends of huge limbs Then the boughs were lopped off, and the cattle could get at the browse. The settlers divided the tree into log, limbs, boughs, and browse. Anything small enough for a cow or deer to masticate was browse. And that is just what you want for a camp in the forest. Not twigs, that may come from a thorn, or boughs, that may be as thick as your wrist, but browse.

And now for a little useless advice. In going into

the woods, don't take a medicine chest or a set of surgical instruments with you. A bit of sticking salve, a vial of painkiller, your fly medicine, and a pair of tweezers, will be enough. Of course you have needles and thread.

If you go before the open season for shooting, take no gun. It will simply be a useless incumbrance and a nuisance.

If you go to hunt, take a solemn oath never to point the shooting end of your gun toward yourself or any other human being.

In still-hunting, swear yourself black in the face never to shoot at a dim, moving object in the woods for a deer, unless you have seen that it is a deer. In these days there are quite as many hunters as deer in the woods; and it is a heavy, wearisome job to pack a dead or wounded man ten or twelve miles out to a clearing, let alone that it spoils all the pleasure of the hunt, and is apt to raise hard feelings among his relations.

In a word, act coolly and rationally. So shall your outing be a delight in conception and the fulfillment thereof; while the memory of it shall come back to you in pleasant dreams, when legs and shoulders are too stiff and old for knapsack and rifle.

That is me. That is why I sit here to-night— with the north wind and sleet rattling the one window of my little den—writing what I hope younger and stronger men will like to take into the woods with them, and read. Not that I am so very old. The youngsters are still not anxious to buck against the muzzleloader in off-hand shooting. But, in common with a thousand other old graybeards, I feel that the fire, the fervor, the steel, that once carried me over the trail from dawn until dark, is dulled and deadened within me.

> We had our day of youth and May ;
> We may have grown a trifle sober ;
> But life may reach a wintry way,
> And we are only in October.

Wherefore, let us be thankful that there are still thousands of cool, green nooks beside crystal springs, where the weary soul may hide for a time, away from debts, duns and deviltries, and a while commune with nature in her undress.

And with kindness to all true woodsmen; and with malice toward none, save the trout-hog, the netter, the cruster, and skin-butcher, let us

PREPARE TO TURN IN.

INDEX.

Index.

A WEEKLY JOURNAL.

The *Forest and Stream* believes in the recreation to be found in the haunts of deer and grouse, and trout and bass. It believes in the common sense that calls a halt in business drive and professional grind, for a holiday with gun, rod and paddle—if only afterward to drive the faster and grind the harder. It is a journal for those who love the country and life out of doors. It reflects the spirit and records the experiences of the great army of outers. If you have any sympathy with these things, the *Forest and Stream* is just the paper you would like to have come into your home every week. The departments are:

Sportsman Tourist,	**The Kennel,**
Natural History,	**Yachting,**
Game Bag and Gun,	**Canoeing,**
Sea and River Fishing.	**Rifle and Trap.**

Its pages contain sketches of travel, adventure and observation at home and abroad, accounts of experience on shooting and fishing excursions, sketches of frontier life, Indian folk lore stories, illustrated articles on American wild animals, papers on the domestication of game, the care and training of dogs, and in short an inexhaustible store of entertaining, wholesome and instructive literature. Send 10 cents for specimen copy. Price, $4.00 per year.

FOREST AND STREAM PUBLISHING CO.,

346 BROADWAY, NEW YORK.